Practicing Organization Development

The Change Agent Series for Groups and Organizations

MISSION STATEMENT

The books in this series are intended to be cutting-edge, state-of-the-art, innovative approaches to organization change and development. They are written for and by practitioners interested in new approaches to facilitating effective organization change. They are geared to providing both theory and advice on practical applications.

SERIES EDITORS

William J. Rothwell
Roland Sullivan
Kristine Quade

EDITORIAL BOARD

David Bradford
W. Warner Burke
Edith Whitfield Seashore
Robert Tannenbaum
Christopher G. Worley
Shaolin Zhang

Other Practicing Organization Development Titles

Rewiring Organizations

for the

Networked

Economy

Rewiring Organizations for the Networked Economy

Organizing, Managing, and Leading in the Information Age

Stan Herman

Editor

Foreword by Richard Beckhard

JOSSEY-BASS/PFEIFFER
A Wiley Company
www.pfeiffer.com

Practicing
Organization
Development

Published by

JOSSEY-BASS/PFEIFFER

A Wiley Company
989 Market Street
San Francisco, CA 94103-1741
415.433.1740; Fax 415.433.0499
800.274.4434; Fax 800.569.0443

| www.pfeiffer.com |

Jossey-Bass/Pfeiffer is a registered trademark of Jossey-Bass Inc., A Wiley Company.

ISBN: 0-7879-6065-9

Library of Congress Cataloging-in-Publication Data

Rewiring organizations for the networked economy : organizing,
managing, and leading in the information age / Stan Herman,
editor.
    p. cm. — (Practicing organization development series)
Includes bibliographical references and index.
  ISBN 0-7879-6065-9 (alk. paper)
  1. Information technology—Management. 2. Management
information systems. 3. Business networks. 4. Electronic
commerce. 5. America Online (Online service). 6. Internet. I.
Herman, Stanley M., 1928- II. Series.
  HD30.2 .R49 2002
  658'.05—dc21

2001006405

We at Jossey-Bass strive to use the most environmentally sensitive paper stocks available to us. Our publications are printed on acid-free recycled stock whenever possible, and our paper always meets or exceeds minimum GPO and EPA requirements.

Acquiring Editor: Josh Blatter   Senior Production Editor: Dawn Kilgore
Director of Development: Kathleen Dolan Davies   Manufacturing Supervisor: Becky Carreño
Developmental Editor: Susan Rachmeler   Interior and Cover Design: Bruce Lundquist
Editor: Rebecca Taff

Printing   10 9 8 7 6 5 4 3 2 1

Contents

Part 2: The New Strategic Basics

Part 3: Collaborative Challenges

Part 5: Conclusions and Implications

10. Re-Evaluating Our Values for a Better Fit   177
Stan Herman

Foreword
to the Series

ON **1967,** Warren Bennis, Ed Schein, and I were faculty members of the Sloan School of Management at MIT. We decided to produce a series of paperback books that collectively would describe the state of the field of organization development (OD). Organization development as a field had been named by me and several others from our pioneer change effort at General Mills in Minneapolis, Minnesota, some ten years earlier.

Today I define OD as "a systemic and systematic change effort, using behavioral science knowledge and skill, to transform the organization to a new state."

In any case, several books and many articles had been written, but there was no consensus on whether OD was a field of practice, an area of study, or a profession. We had not even established OD as a theory or even as a practice.

We decided that there was a need for something that would describe the state of OD. Our intention was to each write a book and also to recruit three other authors. After some searching, we found a young editor who had just joined the small publishing house of Addison-Wesley. We made contact, and the series was born. Our audience was to be human resource professionals who spent their time consulting with managers in their development through various small-group activities, such as team building. More than thirty books have been published in that series, and the series has had a life of its own. We just celebrated its thirtieth anniversary.

At last year's National OD Network Conference, I said that it was time for the OD profession to change and transform itself. Is that not what we change agents tell our clients to do? This new Jossey-Bass/Pfeiffer series will do just that. It can be seen as:

- A documentation of the re-invention of OD;

- An effort that will take us to the next level; and

- A practical effort to transfer to the world the theory and practice of leading-edge practitioners and theorists.

The books in this new series will thus prove to be valuable resources for change agents to keep current with the new and leading-edge ideas and practices.

May this very exciting change agent series be most creative and innovative. May it give our field a renewed burst of energy and awareness.

Richard Beckhard
Written on Labor Day weekend 1999 from my summer cabin near Bethel, Maine

Introduction
to the Series

THERE ARE WATERSHED MOMENTS in history that change everything after them. The attack on Pearl Harbor was one of those. The bombing of Hiroshima was another. The terrorist attack on the World Trade Center in New York City was our most recent. All resulted in significant change that transformed many lives and organizations.

Practicing Organization Development: The Change Agent Series for Groups and Organizations is a series of books that was launched to help those who must cope with or create change. The series is designed for the authors to share what is working or not working, to provoke critical thinking about change, and to offer creative ways to deal with change, rather than the destructive ones noted above.

The Current State of Change Management and Organization Development

Almost as soon as the ink was dry on the first wave of books published in this series, we heard that its focus was too narrow. We heard that the need for theory and practice extended beyond OD into change management. More than one respected authority urged us to reconsider our focus, moving beyond OD to include books on change management generally.

Organization development is not the only way that change can be engineered or coped with in organizational settings. We always knew that, of course. And we remain grounded in the view that change management, however it is carried out, should be based on such values as respect for the individual, participation and involvement in change by those affected by it, and interest in the improvement of organizational settings on many levels—including productivity improvement, but also improvement in achieving work/life balance and in a values-based approach to management and to change.

A Brief History of the Genesis of the Series

A few years ago, and as a direct result of the success of *Practicing Organization Development: A Guide for Practitioners* by Rothwell, Sullivan, and McLean, the publisher—feeling that OD was experiencing a rebirth of interest in the United States and in other nations—wanted to launch a new OD series. The goal of this new series was not to replace, or even to compete directly with, the well-established Addison-Wesley OD Series (edited by Edgar Schein). Instead, as the editors saw it, the series would provide a means by which the most promising authors in OD whose voices had not previously been heard could share their ideas. The publisher enlisted the support of Bill Rothwell, Roland Sullivan, and Kristine Quade to turn the dream of a series into a reality.

This series was long in the making and has been steadily evolving since its inception. The original vision was an ambitious one—and involved no less than reinventing OD and re-energizing interest in the research and practice surrounding it. Sponsoring books was one means to that end.

There were to be others. Indeed, after nearly a year of planning, the editors are pleased to note that the series is hosting a website (www.pfeiffer.com/go/od). Far more than just a place to advertise the series, the site serves as a real-time learning community for OD practitioners. Additionally, the series is hosting a conference, entitled "Practicing Cutting-Edge OD," which is to be held at The Pennsylvania State University in University Park in April 2002 (see www.outreach.psu.edu/C&I/CuttingEdgeOD).

What Distinguishes the Books in This Series

The books in this series are meant to be challenging, cutting-edge, and state-of-the-art in their approach to OD and change management. The goal of the series is to provide an outlet for proven authorities in OD and change management who have not put their ideas into print or for up-and-coming writers in OD and change management who have new, sometimes unorthodox, approaches that are stimulating and exciting. Some books in this series describe inspirational concepts that can lead to actionable change and purvey ideas so new that they are not fully developed.

Unique to this series is the cutting-edge emphasis, the immediate applicability, and the ease of transferability of the concepts. The aim of this series is nothing less than to reinvent, re-energize, and reinvigorate OD and change management. In each book, we have also recommended that the author(s) provide:

- A research base of some kind, meaning new information derived from practice and/or systematic investigation, and

- Practical tools, worksheets, case studies, and other ready-to-go approaches that help the authors drag "theory" to "practice" to make these new, cutting-edge approaches more concrete.

Subject Matter That Will (and Will Not) Be Covered

The books in this series are varied in their approach, but they are united by their focus. All share an emphasis on organization development (OD) and change management (CM). Hence, books in this series are about participative change efforts. They are not about such other popular topics as leadership, management development, consulting, or group dynamics—unless those topics are treated in new, cutting-edge ways and are geared to OD and change management practitioners.

This Book

In *Rewiring Organizations for the Networked Economy,* Stan Herman and his contributors explore a variety of topics related to the fast-paced and constantly connected new economy. This book covers strategy and information technology, virtual teaming, whole system transformation conferences, and the conflict and convergence that HR and IT departments are facing. Also presented is an internal consultant's perspective based on her experiences at AOL. Pulling technology together with organization change and development, Herman concludes the book by taking a look at how values and culture impact, and are impacted by, the networked economy.

William J. Rothwell
University Park, PA

Roland Sullivan
Deephaven, MN

Kristine Quade
Minnetonka, MN

Statement
of the Board

IT IS OUR PLEASURE TO PARTICIPATE in and influence the start-up of *Practicing Organization Development: The Change Agent Series for Groups and Organizations.* The purpose of the series is to stimulate the profession and influence how organization change is defined and practiced. This statement is intended to set the context for the series by addressing three important questions: (1) What are the key issues facing organization change and development in the 21st Century? (2) Where does—or should—OD fit in the field of organization change and development? and (3) What is the purpose of this series?

What Are the Key Issues Facing Organization Change and Development in the 21st Century?

One of the questions is the extent to which leaders can control forces or can only be reactive. Will globalization and external forces be so powerful that they will prevent organizations from being able to "stay ahead of the change curve"? And what will be the role of technology, especially information technology, in the change process? To what extent can it be a carrier of change (as well as a source of change)?

What will the relationship be between imposed change and collaborative change? Will the increased education of the workforce demand the latter, or will the requirement of having to make fundamental changes demand leadership that sets goals that participants would not willingly set on their own? And what is the relationship between these two forms of change?

Who will be the change agent? Is this a separate profession, or will that increasingly be the responsibility of the organization's leaders? If the latter, how does that change the role of the change professional?

What will be the role of values for change in the 21st Century? Will the key values be performance—efficiency and effectiveness? And what role will the humanistic values of more traditional OD play? Or will the growth of knowledge (and human competence) as an organization's core competence make this a moot point in that performance can only occur if one takes account of humanistic values?

What is the relationship between other fields and the area of change? Can any change process that is not closely linked with strategy be truly effective? Can change agents focus only on process, or do they need to be knowledgeable and actively involved in the organization's products/services and understand the market niche in which the organization operates?

Where Does—or Should—OD Fit in the Field of Organization Change and Development?

We offer the following definition of OD to stimulate debate:

> Organization development is a system-wide and values-based collaborative process of applying behavioral science knowledge to the adaptive development, improvement, and reinforcement of such organizational features as the strategies, structures, processes, people, and cultures that lead to organization effectiveness.

The definition suggests that OD can be understood in terms of its several foci:

First, *OD is a system-wide process.* It works with whole systems. In the past, the bias has been toward working at the individual and group levels. More recently, the focus has shifted to organizations and multi-organization systems. We support that trend in general, but honor and acknowledge the fact that the traditional focus on smaller systems is both legitimate and necessary.

Second, *OD is values-based.* Traditionally, OD has attempted to distinguish itself from other forms of planned change and applied behavioral science by promoting a set of humanistic values and by emphasizing the importance of personal growth as a key to its practice. Today, that focus is blurred and there is much debate about the value base underlying the practice of OD. We support a more formal and direct conversation about what these values are and how the field is related to them.

Third, *OD is collaborative.* Our first value commitment as OD practitioners is to bring about an inclusive, diverse workforce with a focus of integrating differences into a world-wide culture mentality.

Fourth, *OD is based on behavioral science knowledge.* Organization development should incorporate and apply knowledge from sociology, psychology, anthropology, technology, and economics toward the end of making systems more effective. We support the continued emphasis in OD on behavioral science knowledge and believe that OD practitioners should be widely read and comfortable with several of the disciplines.

Fifth, *OD is concerned with the adaptive development, improvement, and reinforcement of strategies, structures, processes, people, culture, and other features of organizational life.* This statement describes not only the organizational elements that are the target of change but also the process by which effectiveness is increased. That is, OD works in a variety of areas, and it is focused on improving those areas. We believe that such a statement of process and content strongly implies that a key feature of OD is the transference of knowledge and skill to the system so that it is more able to handle and manage change in the future.

Sixth and finally, *OD is about improving organization effectiveness.* It is not just about making people happy; it is also concerned with meeting financial goals, improving productivity, and addressing stakeholder satisfaction. We believe that OD's future is closely tied to the incorporation of this value in its purpose and the demonstration of this objective in its practice.

This definition raises a host of questions:

- Are OD and organization change and development one and the same, or are they different?
- Has OD become just a collection of tools, methods, and techniques? Has it lost its values?

- Does it talk "systems," but ignore them in practice?

- Are consultants facilitators of change or activists of change?

- To what extent should consulting be driven by consultant value versus holding only the value of increasing the client's effectiveness?

- How can OD practitioners help formulate strategy, shape the strategy development process, contribute to the content of strategy, and drive how strategy will be implemented?

- How can OD focus on the drivers of change external to individuals, such as the external environment, business strategy, organization change, and culture change, as well as on the drivers of change internal to individuals, such as individual interpretations of culture, behavior, style, and mindset?

- How much should OD be part of the competencies of all leaders? How much should it be the sole domain of professionally trained, career-oriented OD practitioners?

What Is the Purpose of This Series?

This series is intended to provide current thinking about organization change and development as a field and to provide practical approaches based on sound theory and research. It is targeted for full-time external or internal change practitioners; top executives in charge of enterprise-wide change; and managers, HR practitioners, training and development professionals, and others who have responsibility for change in organizational and trans-organizational settings. At the same time, these books will be directed toward cutting-edge thinking and state-of-the-art approaches. In some cases, the ideas, approaches, or techniques described are still evolving, so the books are intended to open up dialogue.

We know that the books in this series will provide a leading forum for thought-provoking dialogue within the field.

About the Board Members

David Bradford is senior lecturer in organizational behavior at the Graduate School of Business, Stanford University, Palo Alto, California. He is co-author (with Allan R. Cohen) of *Managing for Excellence, Influence Without Authority,* and *POWER UP: Transforming Organizations Through Shared Leadership.*

W. Warner Burke is professor of psychology and education in the department of organization and leadership at Teachers College at Columbia University in New York. He also serves as a senior advisor to PricewaterhouseCoopers. His most recent publication is *Business Profiles of Climate Shifts: Profiles of Change Makers*, with William Trahant and Richard Koonce.

Edith Whitfield Seashore is an organization consultant and co-founder (with Morley Segal) of AUNTL Masters Program in Organization Development. She is co-author of *What Did You Say?* and *The Art of Giving and Receiving Feedback* and co-editor of *The Promise of Diversity*.

Robert Tannenbaum is emeritus professor of development of human systems, Graduate School of Management, University of California, Los Angeles, and recipient of the Lifetime Achievement Award by the National OD Network. He has published numerous books, including *Human Systems Development* (with Newton Margulies and Fred Massarik).

Christopher G. Worley is director, MSOD Program, Pepperdine University, Malibu, California. He is co-author of *Organization Development and Change* (7th ed.), with Tom Cummings, and of *Integrated Strategic Change,* with David Hitchin and Walter Ross.

Shaolin Zhang is senior manager of organization development for Motorola (China) Electronics Ltd. He received his master's degree in American Studies from Beijing Foreign Studies University, Beijing, China, and holds a Ph.D. in sociology from York University, Toronto, Ontario.

This book is first dedicated to its authors and their varied and venturesome points of view. It is also dedicated to NELA, the New Edge Leadership Alliance. NELA's premise is that information technology is changing the world, thereby fundamentally changing the way we need to manage, lead, and organize. NELA's intention is to encourage the examination of emerging management theory and practice and to contribute to the flow of ideas and methods. The NELA website may be viewed at www.newedgeleadership.com/

Acknowledgments

OUR THANKS ARE EXTENDED to and deserved by all of those, too many to list, who wrote in books and online about the subjects we examine here, as well as others whose conversations and critiques helped us to focus more clearly on what needed to be said. The series editors, Roland Sullivan, Bill Rothwell, and Kristine Quade, also played major parts in bringing the book together. In addition, the editor has some special debts to the following people, who contributed their time and advice as the book went through its long birthing process:

Patrick Ahern, my associate and editorial question asker;

Georgia Herman, my wife and feisty critic; and

Susan Rachmeler, the book's guide through pre-publication's stringent rituals, who helped me (beyond the call of duty) at some critical junctures.

Preface

Every now and then evolution jumps.

A FEW WEEKS AGO, I heard a thirty-five-year-old attorney, at the height of her career, talk about her feelings of insecurity. She worried because there were young people at her firm in their early twenties who might be able to do her job better than she could. That was because they seemed to have a "natural ability" to access information on the Internet faster and more thoroughly than she did! I felt sympathy for her and, I must admit, some envy of the twenty-year-olds. But then a few days later I heard two colleagues discussing their under-fifteen daughters (both "A" students) who seemed to be able to talk on the telephone and simultaneously conduct "chat-room" conversations on their laptops with twenty or more friends while doing their homework and listening to music! My colleagues wondered aloud whether this ability to "multiplex" (parallel processing of several interweaving thought streams) had been learned or whether the brains of this newer generation had just been "wired" differently.

As part of an introduction to this book, it seems a brief description of my own "evolutionary jump" and how it came about would be in order. About five or six years ago, I had reached a point where I thought that I deserved a bit of a pause in my thirty-year career as a manager and management consultant in the field of change management. To be frank, I had also grown a bit weary with what seemed to me a continual repackaging of longstanding, conventional ideas, theories, and practices. It seemed to me that not much had changed in this field of change management since the 1970s. I began drifting away from this subject and on to other things. And then about three years ago in conversations with some young "techies"—including my son—I suddenly encountered what some called the "new economy" and others called the "networked economy." For the first time in my thirty-plus years of studying and working with organizations, something really was changing—and changing in a seismic way.

I joined a number of other interested colleagues, and we began to think about, talk about, and investigate the changes. Some of those colleagues are authors of chapters in this book.

This is a book that deals with the direct and indirect impacts of information technology as they affect organizing, managing, and leading people in the early 21st Century. Its chapters present a mosaic of experiences and observations by a group of writers who have experienced many of the effects of the hyper-speed information age (some might call it the information age invasion) and who have learned some significant lessons they believe are worth sharing.

Rewiring Organizations for the Networked Economy is directed to those who have recently become involved in leading others (and themselves as well) in adapting to and taking advantage of the often new and unfamiliar realities of this age. We speak especially to those in organizations that are in the early stages of transitioning to the "new economy." We address the effects of information technology on how organizations operate—the new structures, processes, and attitudes that are required of them. The authors aim to make the changes clear and reveal some fresh and compelling new paradigms, as well as the methods, attitudes, and tools for responding to the seismic shifts in 21st Century ideas about organizations and the people who live within them.

How This Book Is Organized

There are five sections to this book. Part 1 provides an overview of what we call the "derived imperatives" of information technology—its profound and inescapable effects on the processes of organizing and managing people. We note that some of our long-held and cherished beliefs about the organizing and managing functions no longer apply. Instead, the impacts of almost instant information handling and distribution and the almost unlimited potential for "connectedness" between organizations and knowledge workers require expansion and extension of our perspectives. We must learn to learn new things quickly and to hold those learnings lightly—ever ready to let them go in favor of yet another more advanced perception.

In Part 2, The New Strategic Basics, we focus on a new paradigm for strategy formulation and implementation. We present a radical revision in our long-cherished notions about the central importance of long-range prediction and planning. They are too limiting for the new economy. Our futures are neither predictable nor controllable. What the new economy demands of us is that we (1) continually sense and evaluate our organization's "ecology" (the dynamics of its interaction with its environment) and (2) respond speedily to new and unanticipated opportunities and problems. We examine the practices of some trail-setting organizations and explain the uses of information technology to facilitate "strategic conversations" that continually update the organization's concentration points.

Part 3, Collaborative Challenges, deals with how the networked economy affects the way people work together. Virtual teaming and whole-system involvement are discussed, with a concentration at the tactical level. How to make the networked economy work in organizations is illustrated by actual cases, models, and techniques.

Part 4, HR, OD, and Information Technology, presents a comprehensive array of basic information technology resources that consultants and others responsible for guiding organization transition efforts will find useful. We also point out that job roles and responsibilities can be radically altered as technology and business needs give birth to new mixtures of functions. Both technical and human organizational skills are being combined in previously unforeseen ways.

Part 5, Conclusions and Implications, addresses some of the more subtle but no less impactful consequences of the networked economy as they influence our values and raise dilemmas about human functioning in an increasingly technology dominated society. Should we fight the trend or join it? Will it control us, or we it, or will our synthesis be an unpredicted third alternative?

Part 1
Setting the Stage

(1)

From "Prediction" to "Emergence"
A New Fundamental

Stan Herman

THE NEW ECONOMY* has lost its magic charm. Alas, it appears among economies to be as mortal as the rest and hasn't transcended the basic laws of all economies. It has had its meteoric rise and its lead-weight descent. It will probably have more of both in the future. But if you think it will go away, if you just ignore it long enough, you are in for problems. At its simplest level, the networked economy is about two things: almost instantaneous information exchange and almost unlimited "connectedness." Except in the smallest, simplest, and most local organizations, one can no more afford to ignore those conditions than one could ignore

---

*In this book we will be using the terms "new economy" and "networked economy" almost interchangeably—using the former when referring to marketplace situations and the latter when dealing with information exchange processes.

the telephone when it first became a part of the business scene in the early years of the 20th Century.

At its epicenter is information technology, but radiating from that source are multiple secondary effects (we call them "derived imperatives") that significantly influence organizing and management principles and that threaten to fracture many of the conventional premises, theories, and practices that have been applied to organizations in the last half of the 20th Century. In short, for the last fifty or more years we tried to make organization management into a science, founded on a set of proven theories and predictable futures that can be controlled. And now—in response to the irresistible forces of information technology and a globalized economy—we are moving into a period of what can best be described as "indeterminacy." We have to accept as a given that, because of the speed and variability of what happens in and among organizations and the society, accurate prediction and control of the future are no longer real options. We need, instead, to learn to adjust and adapt to a continual stream of unforeseeable events that emerges before us. First, two fundamentals.

Uncertainty Is Unavoidable

The organizations of the new economy really are different. They are because the conduits of information technology, and particularly the Internet, are unique media:

- They enable instant globe-wide communication, including the ability to sustain organized project work twenty-four hours a day;

- They have almost unlimited capacity to get, store, and find information;

- They have almost unlimited potential for analyzing and synthesizing information and for turning it into value-added knowledge;

- They allow direct contact with each individual end user (of a product or service) as well as of selected groupings of end users; and

- Each participant has the potential to interact with an almost infinite number of other persons and groups.

In the hyper competition of the new economy, these conditions require organizations to be faster at analysis, choice, and decision making and more connected to customers, suppliers, their industries, and among their own (sometimes geographically dispersed) personnel than ever before. And partially because of these conditions, and the "complexity" that accompanies them, accurately predicting or designing the long-term futures of new economy organizations has become just about impossible. One may reflect nostalgically on the motto of the classical executive who wanted "no surprises," but, like it or not, there will be surprises aplenty.

Technology and Commerce Are the Key Drivers of Organization Change

Organization change forces changes in the premises, values, and methods that are relevant to people working in organizations. This has been so since mankind's earliest times. Agriculture, one of our earliest technologies, changed us from nomadic hunter-gatherers to stable grain-growers. The production of agriculture surpluses enabled the birth of cities. Equally important, freed from the needs to hunt or grow their own food, many people were enabled to perform specialized tasks in metalworking, art, pottery, stone masonry, and so on. Thus, civilization was fundamentally changed.

Later in history, Greek ships carried not only their goods but also their gods through the Mediterranean and profoundly affected the cultures of the lands with which they traded. Railroads tied together national identities (and created national consumerism). The atom bomb initiated the Cold War and the polarization of world power.

We believe that the advent of the information technology age is on par with these other "technology shifts." Each major shift accompanies both direct and secondary changes (that is, in social mores and values, economics, organizational premises, and so forth). For a provocative example, one could make the case that the sexual revolution (in the United States) began with mass-produced cars (and the privacy they offered young Americans). One could then add that birth control pills won the revolution—and changed basic morality. It is interesting to contemplate the future effects of new technologies such as cloning, robotics, and virtual reality, to name just a few, on our lifestyles and norms.

Information technology presents us directly with the gifts of hyper speed and unlimited connectedness. But there are no "free lunches." Information technology also challenges us with its "derived imperatives"—the things we will have to change in our structures, processes, and in human behavior in order to adapt to information technology's potential. It also confronts us with continuing questions about which of our "humanistic values" we are unwilling to adapt and how hard we are willing to struggle to maintain them.

Three Imperatives of Change
Derived from Information Technology

In this first chapter, I'll identify three of what seem to me to be the most important changes—emergence, discontinuous change, and virtual teams—and their implications for how leaders, managers, knowledge workers, and consultants in the new economy will operate. We will discuss each of them briefly in this introduction and they will be explored at some length by this book's authors.

- *Emergence.* Predictive strategies are being replaced by emergent strategies. Emergence requires expanding the functions and styles of leadership and management significantly.

- *Discontinuous Change.* The speed and connection of information and people throughout the globe is now so great as to be a "change in kind" rather than a change in degree. We can no longer depend on gradualism (for example, continuous improvement of existing concepts and processes) as a viable principle for organization success. Our times require abrupt departures from past practice—new concepts for structuring, organizing, and processing work.

- *Virtual Teams.* Virtual teams are increasing in importance, and this requires fundamental changes in the ways we view and work with members of these dispersed/distributed groups, as collectives and as individuals.

Emergence

In *New Rules for the New Economy,* Kevin Kelly (1999) says, "Unlike the industrial era's relatively simple environment, in which it was fairly clear what an optimal product looked like and where on the stable horizon a company should place itself, it is increasingly difficult in the network economy to discern what hills are highest and which summits are false. . . . Trails are riddled with dead ends, lead to false summits, and [are] made impassable by big-time discontinuities." We have recently felt the accuracy of Kelly's forecast with more impact than even he might have imagined, as legions of software and Web-based commercial companies, large and small, succumb to the realities of pressure for profits.

Microsoft's Bill Gates (1999) says the following about how to cope with the uncertainty and ambiguity: "The goal is to make business reflex nearly instantaneous and to make strategic thought an ongoing, iterative process—not something done every twelve to eighteen months, separate from the daily flow of business."

In the industrial era, leaders and managers attempted to come as close as possible to making their businesses predictable. The business culture has prized careful planning and gradual development of programs and products. Analytical business forecasting, and programs like TQM and other quality-oriented efforts, concentrated on avoiding or reducing errors. But the new economy favors speed over caution. Kirby Dyess (1999), vice president for business development at Intel, cites "Fail fast and re-invent" as its slogan. Thorough analysis and preparation give way to Gates' (1999) aim to make information and reaction, "nearly instantaneous."

In the industrial era, we viewed strategic planning as a logical and linear process, an exercise of reasoning and will. The five-year plan was to take us to our pre-planned future in prescribed steps. But in the new economy we recognize that a five-year-out destination, even if we could reach it, would probably be out of date by the time we got there. In a world as turbulent as ours, a company CEO in the book-publishing industry may wake up one morning to find that his principal competition is coming not from within the industry but from a software producer who provides books online—and can do it faster and cheaper. Envisioning and planning are not dead yet, and we need to be careful in our enthusiasm not to play any premature dirges. "Plan ahead" is still a slogan of some use, but a limited one. First, organizations need the capacity for continual adaptation to changes in their total "ecologies"—not just in their industries. Then "envisioning" and planning need to be conducted in a more fluid and short-cycle context.

If the key strategic concepts of the old economy were prediction (of the future) and prescription (of the discrete steps for reaching the objective), the new economy's keys involve being prepared for the emergence (of the future) and convergence (of the required person power, technology, and resources to respond fast and well). In our planning, we need to cultivate a breadth of view that enables us to access multiple paths, choose from among them, and keep open as many options as we can manage, but not more than that.

Strategic navigation—a term I first heard from Richard Hames, who authors a chapter on this subject—is the ability to steer an organization as it moves through unpredictable waters. As Carol Willett, author of a chapter on virtual teams, says, "It's like the trim tab on a rudder—we adjust it to reinforce what's desirable in our course and steer away from what's not."

Catch the Wave, Ride It, Catch Another One

Western mankind has traditionally, and in a deep cultural sense, made the assumption that equilibrium and stability are the rule in life and that turbulence and discontinuity are the dysfunctional exceptions. Our classic model for managing organization change involved first, deliberately "unfreezing" the system, second, accomplishing our planned revisions, and third, "re-freezing" the system. But in this new era, those assumptions do not seem to apply. As Bill Gates (1999) puts it, "punctuated chaos" rather than "punctuated equilibrium" is now the rule.

Speaking here to those consultants and leaders who are responsible for change management, we suggest the following as a new economy perspective: Change is a continual and inescapable fact of organization existence. The character of change is inevitably the result of the intersection of preparatory intentions (planning) and unanticipated events (reality). The core competency of change consultants is not so much planning change but rather facilitating human interaction around a targeted effort within an ever-changing universe.

Finally, perhaps the most stubborn assumption of the old economy has been that there is, or must be, one right way of organizing and managing. Management theoreticians have been searching for it, developing their various versions of it, and "selling" it for much of the 20th Century, and Western business organizations and economies have benefited from their efforts. But in this new century, there are a number of "right ways" depending on each situation.

The following quotes from well-acknowledged leaders and observers of the networked economy form the vanguard of an ever-lengthening parade of those who lead our organizations into this new era.

- "[The best strategists have] a feel for the business not unlike a potter's feel for the clay. . . . By seeing patterns take shape in their environments, the best strategists find strategies as well as create them. . . . Appropriate strategic planning for our times is convergent: A single action can be taken, feedback can be received and the process can continue until the organization converges on the pattern that becomes its strategy" (Mintzberg, 1996).

- "Strategy requires debunking orthodoxy, defining competence, exploiting discontinuity—understanding the revolutionary potential of what is already happening" (Hamel, 1998).

- "Managers need a new way to think about managing change in today's knowledge organization. . . . Managers need to think in terms of overseeing a dynamic. Managing change is like balancing a mobile" (Daniel-Duck, 1993).

- "The world changes too fast, making detailed plans obsolete before you can implement them. . . . Far better than a precise plan is a clear sense of direction and compelling beliefs" (Waldrop, 2000).

Guideline: Emergence

Leadership in the new economy is like riding a surfboard. You need to

- Sense the territory for emerging opportunities and hazards;

- Respond rapidly with converged effort and resources;

- Innovate and keep moving; and

- Maintain your balance in a rhythm between emergence and convergence (focusing sufficient attention and resources to accomplish a result)

while encouraging others to do the same.

Discontinuous Change

A number of terms—"discontinuous change" or "sea change," for example—have been used in statistics and social science to portray a degree and speed of change that is so great and sudden as to constitute an actual break with past trends. Imagine, for example, a gradually rising mathematical trend line that suddenly jumps vertical (a step-function increase). Information technology has produced that kind of change. According to *The Wall Street Journal* (2001), the Internet is making its way into American homes faster than any prior major technology: Electricity took forty-six years to reach 25 percent of U.S. homes, the telephone took thirty-five years, and the personal computer took sixteen years. The World Wide Web took only seven years. The estimates now are that 72 percent of households will have access to the Web by 2005. While these are impressive numbers, they deal only with those directly connected to the Internet industry. They do not take into account the huge proportion of "old economy" companies, government, and service organizations that are inextricably linked to one another through the electronic exchange of information on a global basis.

Why is information technology, and particularly the Internet, a truly unique medium? A report by investment advisors Harris, Bretall, Sullivan, and Smith (2001) points out the following:

- Information technology is instantly global;

- It allows direct contact with each end user (of a product or service);

- It has no limitation of "shelf space" for information/knowledge products; and we would add

- Users are only one click away from transacting.

The eventual aim of the information systems designers is a "seamless" connective process that provides all the relevant information necessary to each and every part of the organization—almost instantly—from sales through production to new design. Wal-Mart has for some time possessed an inventory system that features the seamless characteristic, available not only within the company but to its suppliers as well. GE, too, among others, has created electronic networks linking its internal operations with those of suppliers—saving time and inventory costs. One noteworthy characteristic of GE's system is that it requires all product managers to respond to customer questions within forty-eight hours or the question is passed on to the manager's boss (*Business Week,* 1999).

New Structures—Often Fuzzy

These new capacities for "almost instantaneous" information transfer come with their own derived imperatives. For example, these derived imperatives make obsolete old ideas about chains of command. They are no longer sufficient (nor are ideas to eliminate hierarchy entirely). Conventional notions about information secrecy and proprietary safeguards need to be balanced against free-flowing information exchange. Just as "seamless" is one key word of the new economy, "transparency" is another. Generally, it is more important to get relevant information to people quickly and enable them to exchange that information among themselves than it is to safeguard it. The proliferation of organization "intranets" (specialized internal versions of the Internet) is evidence of business translation of information dispersion into practical action.

Nevertheless, getting information to people quickly is of little use unless they have the ability to understand its significance and the power to use it in making their contribution to the value chain. To serve this purpose, leading organizations have for some time been moving from the "silo" model of stable, top-down, functional hierarchies to new patterns of organizing that are temporary, often cross-functional, and varied to suit the ecology in which the organization currently operates. Two of the most interesting of the new forms are "hubs," which Henry Mintzberg (Mintzberg & Van der Heyden, 1999) describes as "a coordinating center" at which people, things, or information move. A hub can be a person, such as a manager or coach, or a building, or even a core competence of an organization "such as optics at Canon or bonding and coating at 3M," according to Mintzberg. "Webs" are another of the new forms, especially applicable in the Internet context. A web is a grid of relationships without a coordinating center. All parts of the web connect to all other parts, at least potentially, and enable cross-exchanges of information, points of view, and recommendations for action to be taken.

Scuttlebutt Around the Water Cooler
Hasn't Gone Away, It's Just Gone Electronic

Once again though, these new forms are not without risks and costs. Those charged with responsibility for performance and profits in organizations are presented with great opportunities, but they are counterpoised against real dilemmas. For example, consider the following, reported February 19, 2000, by Reuters:

▶ Faster Web Connections
Prompt More Surfing at Work

NEW YORK—Much to the chagrin of many managers and supervisors, people are spending more time surfing the Internet at work than they are at home, mainly because home Web connection speeds pale in comparison to the faster connections that companies give their employees. ◀

Another example involves a very large company we know of that developed an intranet for 5,000 of its engineers on three continents with the expectation that the intranet would foster the exchange of task-centered knowledge among them. While some of this occurred, what was equally noteworthy was that a great many of the engineers set up their own personal websites, and their exchanges contained much personal communication that, as the company saw it, was irrelevant to their work. Problems of "misuse" of company computers by employees for outside interests are acknowledged to be widespread. Many companies have set up elaborate regulations and monitoring programs to prevent these perceived misuses. Some others have accepted the practices as part of the "learning experience" and seem to be hoping for the best.

Wide dissemination of authority seems to be no more an unmixed blessing than the dissemination of information. One of the most commonly heard complaints is that it takes too long and too much work to come to a consensus-based decision among a large group of people with diverse backgrounds and self-interests. Another is that consensus decisions, when they are made, are often compromises that lack the boldness and imaginative power of those made by single dedicated and inspired individuals or self-selecting combinations of such individuals. These problems are exacerbated significantly when we deal with virtual teams, composed of people who have little if any face-to-face contact and are often from a mixture of countries and cultures. Consider the model presented by MIT's "Initiative on Inventing the Organizations of the 21st Century":

▶ The Dawn of the E-Lance Economy

"A world in which business . . . is carried out autonomously by independent contractors connected through personal computers and electronic networks. These electronically connected freelancers—e-lancers—would join together into fluid and temporary networks to produce and sell goods and services. When the job is done—after a day, a month, a year—the network would dissolve and its members would again become independent agents" (Malone & Laubacher, 1999). ◀

For this model or others comparable to it to work well, we will need to learn a good deal more about the effects of information technology on people interaction and vice versa. For now we can provide a few general guidelines that seem to make sense.

Guidelines: Discontinuous Change

The goal is to connect organizations, people, and information by doing the following:

- Speed knowledge transfer;

- Create quick feedback loops;

- Develop partners and allies;

- Bet on the net—use the technology;

- Focus first on your "ecology"—the environment within which your organization operates—then on how well your organization fits;

- Beware of the competence trap—getting too good at things that are no longer relevant; and

- Befriend uncertainty and navigate within it.

Virtual Teams

"Although estimates vary widely, some 30 million to 40 million people in the United States are now either telecommuters or home-based workers," according to Mahlon Apgar IV, vice president of Booz Allen & Hamilton, Inc. What motivates top management to enable this new phenomenon? According to Apgar (1998), the four reasons listed below are paramount:

- Cost reduction (since 1991, AT&T has saved $550 million in cash flow and IBM more than $100 million annually in its North American sales and distribution unit alone);

- The potential to increase productivity;

- The possibility of keeping talented, highly motivated employees who might not otherwise remain; and

- Opportunities to capture government incentives and avoid costly sanctions.

Virtual work groups are increasing because they are a product of the derived imperatives of speed and connectedness. Globalized virtual groups offer the 24/7/365 response better than any other option. Working in "shifts" according to their time zones, virtual groups have the capacity to continue working on a project twenty-four hours a day, seven days a week, 365 days a year. The shift to virtual groups is also stimulated by the geographic spread of talents the networked economy is able to access. No longer are technologists bunched in exclusive enclaves like Silicon Valley. As an employer, you can find them in an increasing number of countries from Ireland to India, and often for less money!

Terry Armstrong, who has studied virtual teams for several years, cites a 1996 study showing that nearly three-fifths of the companies surveyed reported the use of global (virtual) teams (Alex, 1996). Carol Willett of the Applied Knowledge Group, Inc., has, with her colleagues, spent almost thirty years forming and leading globally dispersed virtual teams held together by the USG (precursor to e-mail). In our conversations, she pointed out that "With only the occasional backup of telephone or face-to-face meetings, these folks had to figure out how to discover people's talents, sort out their motivations, provide direction and tasking, play to their strengths, and orchestrate collaborative efforts—all via text (this was before you could send pictures electronically)."

Both Armstrong and Willett agree that the models and processes for effective operations are significantly different between in-person and virtual teams. Armstrong says, "Some managers seem to think that going to virtual teams involves little more than connecting computers and loading the groupware." Some are also relieved by their assumption that the electronic interchange pretty much eliminates the messy people problems they used to have to deal with. They are likely to be disappointed. There is more to team effectiveness than the mechanics (just as there is more to good face-to-face teamwork). The complexity is that we still have to concentrate on the human-to-human interface, even though it is mediated by technology.

Most virtual team issues fall into three categories:

1. Group cohesion and morale building;

2. Establishing individual identity; and

3. Interaction processes that will contribute to effective performance.

Group Cohesion and Morale Building

Building cohesion among work group members who are very often temporary, work in dispersed locations, and almost never see each other is a daunting task. Building morale among international groups seems even more difficult. Perhaps one fundamental problem in building cohesion arises when we, North Americans, make the assumption (often unconsciously) that our prevailing norms and values are "best" or "right" for other nationalities and cultures. For example, North Americans often see arguments between team members as a negative condition, a departure from collaboration, which is the desired state for teamwork. Not so for the Israelis, who, according to an Israeli colleague, believe arguments are healthy contributions to developing optimum solutions. While consultants to U.S. companies frequently advocate increased flexibility and self-determination for U.S. workers, in many third-world organizations, what is most important is to impart the need for reinforcing regularized hours and work habits among the workforce.

Motivation by money and other tangible awards and rewards will become increasingly complicated. There are, of course, many motivating factors for team participation: Some thrive on the challenge, some like the independence of the work, and some like having responsibility to a team. But in U.S. culture, none of these is likely to sustain the interests and energies of employees for the long-term without adequate compensation. There will need to be multiple pay systems that can respond to the performance of both individuals and the group. The current trend toward widespread distribution of stock options and other rewards based on overall business profits will probably continue and may stimulate positive morale among participants when the market is up but gloom and grumbles among the fainthearted when it goes down. The creative use of streaming video productions, especially entertaining "infomercials" that get both general company information and specific project information across to workers, may become a major morale builder as well as a communication tool.

Establishing Individual Identity

There seems to be a fundamental need for most people to establish a personal identity and to be a respected presence among their peers. Achieving that in face-to-face groups probably depends as much on appearance, how one speaks, and personality style—how one "presents" oneself in meetings—as it does on the content quality of one's work. But what happens when appearance, speech, and style are no longer visible? Anecdotal indications are that personalities may change substantially between face-to-face and Internet environments. For example, some people who are reticent and almost "invisible" in conventional meetings become major participants, even leaders, when the medium of presentation becomes the Internet. Others, who are major influences in person, fade to the background because they have less skill with the computer-transmitted written word. The example we gave earlier of the engineers who set up their own home pages on the company intranet seems clearly an effort to create a representation of personal identity—a kind of virtual self.

From the standpoint of each virtual team member, there are also new and puzzling issues. How does one express oneself effectively and "read" others' reactions when there are no feedback clues from faces, bodies, or even voice tones? What styles of written communication are best—should it all be carefully courteous, avoiding any emotional expression that might offend? (Any who have been involved in sustained interchanges on the Internet will recognize how little it takes for someone "out there" to feel offended.)

But what happens when the politeness and politically correct mode become the highest priority? Does that outlaw spontaneity and authenticity and obfuscate substantive argument to the detriment of clarity and the possibilities of creative controversy? We believe that there is a need for virtual teams to develop what the CEO of one software company called an "etiquette" that sets down an agreed-to list of guidelines for avoiding hostility, but that still enables reasonable controversy conducted with civility.

Interaction Processes That Will Contribute to Effective Performance

For the leader or manager responsible for a virtual team, too, the problems of ambiguity complicate the job. As we discussed earlier, the classic model of hierarchical top-down direction has less applicability in an era that requires quick and knowledgeable action by those closest to the situation. That is also true in virtual teams. One advantage the virtual team manager has is that she can, as she desires, have access to the same information as the team members in equally real time. But she probably does not have the specialized knowledge the team members have, nor the time, to become as deeply involved in specific problems as they do.

Emily Post, Miss Manners, and the Flamers: A Recommendation

When we spoke about the individual, we said that balance was needed between our efforts to discourage "hostile" exchanges and enabling the authenticity of fully engaged argument (that excludes personal attack). We suggested that new models of "etiquette" were needed. One of the resources we believe needs to be developed in electronic format is a basic "Etiquette for Virtual Teamwork"—a collection of guidelines that each team can use as a starting point for creating its own unique version. For example, in an Internet-based organization of which I am a member, we have an unwritten guideline that solicits any member's complaint or issue as long as it is accompanied by a clear statement of "what the 'complainer' wants more of, less of, or different" from one or more other members in order to relieve the complaint. This process then provides clear grounds for the parties involved to negotiate. It would be a process that enables the team members to come to a consensus on their own "rules of the game." This is more likely to work than policies and regulations passed down from the top. Management can lend its weight to the guidelines and should also have the right of veto when necessary. Some of the subjects the "V-T Etiquette" might cover include how to disagree without flaming and becoming disagreeable, how to get clarity on the mission and objectives, best ways to advise, get advice, say thank you, let people know you want them to move faster/slower/in a different direction, and so on.

It would also provide opportunities and guidelines for building Internet friendships and communities and the principles and practices for "taking care of yourself" in e-interactions. Finally, all participating would be helped to recognize that this is an early stage in virtual team usage and, just as with the introduction of other new organization forms, much will need to be worked out through trial and error. A good helping of patience and tolerance of others' ways can't hurt as we find our way along.

To close this chapter, we offer a set of questions for discussion that can help organization leaders and their consultants to obtain useful indicators of what is needed to improve the effectiveness of their own organizations' virtual teams. Later, two chapters in this book will cover specific methods for addressing the needs.

▶ Virtual Teams: A Readiness Assessment

Group Cohesion and Morale Building

1. Are leaders and managers clear about currently existing cultural (that is, national, religious, regional) differences and similarities among team members? (Don't assume "we're all the same" or that we even want to be! Find out about cultural tendencies by observing, reading, and asking. If you're a consultant, act as an ombudsman, interpreter, and sounding board for group members. Unless the group will be together a long time, don't work on installing "culture change.")

2. Does the organization use meaningful recognition, money, and other tangible awards and rewards as important motivators? Are pay systems responsive to the performance of both individuals and the group in the balance you want?

3. Are there accepted pathways (for example, e-mail, intranet, phone) for people to exchange casual information and to interact on a personal level? Are there guidelines for what is and is not acceptable dialogue (for example, a shared and explicit etiquette)?

Establishing Individual Identity

4. Does the "information exchange system" provide a way for individuals to establish a personal identity and to become a respected presence among their peers?

5. Over time, are the communication patterns of team members becoming more comfortable, authentic, and effective? Or are they becoming antagonistic, evasive, and scattered?

6. Does the organization pay attention to emerging issues that may be particular to virtual workers (for example, the effects of rapid and frequent revisions of strategic objectives communicated via e-mail on employees' sense of clarity about how and where their work fits into the strategic big picture)?

Interaction Processes That Will Contribute to Effective Performance

7. Does the team have the leadership and the managership it needs? If not, does it flounder—lack focus, fail to meet commitments, and so on—or is it too tightly controlled—too procedure-bound, too many approval levels required, etc.?

8. Do organization units recognize the importance of learning how to make virtual teaming work and communicating their learnings to other parts of the organization? ◄

As this book continues, it will address a number of these potential issues and others that seem continually to spring forth in unpredictable ways for our new era organizations. At the same time, in a larger sense, this book can only scratch the surface of possibilities. Just as in the past, with the advent of other discontinuous changes—the telephone, automobile, railroads—we work and live on the cusp of new potentials for good and for ill, and it is often difficult to tell which is which. We, who are the authors of this book, hold as our fondest hope that many of its readers will join us in exploring and helping to shape the future of the networked economy. To facilitate that purpose, we ask you to contact the editor, Stan Herman, at Stan@NewEdgeLeadership.com.

References

Alex, R. (1996). *Identifying virtual teams.* Unpublished study.

Apgar, M., IV. (1998, May/June). The alternative workplace: Changing where and how people work. *Harvard Business Review.*

Business Week. (1999, April 5). Available: www.businessweek.com

Crainer, S. (2000). *The management century.* San Francisco: Jossey-Bass.

Daniel-Duck, J. (1993, November 1). The art of balancing. *Harvard Business Review.*

Drucker, P. (1999). *Management challenges for the 21st century.* New York: Harper-Business.

Dyess, K. (1999, July 15). *Emerging issues for organizations.* Speech presented at the Pepperdine University MSOD Program Conference, Malibu, California.

Gates, B. (1999). *Business at the speed of thought.* New York: Warner.

Hamel, G. (1998). *Thought leaders: Insights on the future of business.* New York: Booz Allen & Hamilton.

Harris, Bretall, Sullivan & Smith. (2001). Available: http://www.hbss.com.

Kelly, K. (1999). *New rules for the new economy.* New York: Penguin.

Kurtzman, J. (1999). *Insights on the future of business.* San Francisco: Jossey-Bass.

Malone, T.W., & Laubacher, R.J. (1999). *Initiative on inventing the organizations of the 21st century.* Cambridge, MA: Massachusetts Institute of Technology.

Mintzberg, H. (1996, July 1). Musings on management. *Harvard Business Review.*

Mintzberg, H., & Van der Heyden, L. (1999, September/October). Organigraphs: Drawing how companies really work. *Harvard Business Review.*

Waldrop, M.M. (2000, August). Dee Hock on organizations. *Fast Company.*

Wall Street Journal. (2001, February 12), p. 16.

Part 2
The New Strategic Basics

ⒷEFORE OUR EYES a discontinuity is being thrust upon us that challenges our long-cherished notions about the central importance of long-range planning. From an emphasis on predicting and controlling our organizational futures we must shift to the derived imperative of "emergence." Our futures are neither predictable nor controllable. What the new economy demands of us is that we recognize the primacy of (1) continual sensing of our organization's "ecology" (the dynamics of its interaction with its environment) and (2) the requirement for rapid responsiveness to new problems and opportunities. We must be able, when required, to "try it out—fail quick—and re-invent."

And even as we broaden our awareness of what is developing in our ecology, executives are more than ever required to make contingent choices (*rather than final decisions*) about where and how their organizations will focus their always-limited resources of people and money. Further, these choices must be communicated in sufficient clarity for those who will be responsible for implementing to understand and perform. Thus, the challenge to management—to continually review existing priorities, to adjust them, to communicate changes rapidly, and, perhaps most important, to patiently and purposefully condition those responsible for doing the work so that they can accept these often abrupt changes in direction as necessary and normal. In other words, keep everyone in the organization light on their feet!

On the other side of the coin, the challenge to working-level implementers is to focus on their assigned tasks and at the same time be prepared to veer quickly to new ones, with a minimum of confusion and without undue frustration. These are formidable challenges indeed. Dealing with them requires balanced judgment and a more sophisticated level of business and market understanding at all organization levels. It also calls for more authentic two-way exchanges that enable people to speak to and hear each other at levels of frankness that transcend levels of hierarchy.

In this section we also see how the new networked economy demands a "bias for action" more than a careful five-year plan and how some trail-setting organizations have responded. New concepts and practices that work in delivering close-to-immediate strategic action are presented. Working in the context of complexity theory, Richard Hames describes a dynamic adaptive system used by the Australian Internal Revenue Service that captures people's involvement through a special organization (the "Change Brain") within the organization. This group continually updates strategic aims and the supporting tactics they require.

Bill Bruck describes the uses of information technology to facilitate "strategic conversations" for continual updating by those involved. And he points out that "These conversations are increasingly technology conversations: They are conversations about technology, and they are conversations that are mediated by technology."

In the last chapter of this section, Mary Foley takes us beyond the typically idealized and sanitized versions of how companies operate to some "hard-nosed" observations from the inside and shows us what is really central to a company's purpose and the problems as well as the advantages that come from actual operations.

Strategic Navigation
Learning Viability
in a World Wired for Speed

Richard Hames

ⓞRGANIZATIONS ARE BUILT TO LAST. Buildings, strategies, systems, hierarchies, processes, and protocols are all designed to ensure longevity of the enterprise. Or are they? There comes a time when even the most incomparable and elegant of designs no longer fulfils its original intention. What if our assumptions regarding effective strategic management are simply obsolete? What if the very focus, structures, and mechanisms designed to ensure high performance, corporate sustainability, innovation, and best practice actually achieve the opposite? What happens if we ignore long-term viability in favor of short-term profit?

Clearly, the implications for managing contemporary organizations in real time are profound. Just as important though, is ensuring their long-term viability. "Viability" means being self-sustaining over time. But it is only possible to remain viable if we intimately connect our inside and outside worlds in ways that promote learning, responsiveness, and adaptiveness. In the dot-com world of the knowledge economy, insistence on relevance to a historically established core purpose is not a criterion for viability. Nor are cutting-edge technologies, low-cost marketing, or being a high-value-added producer or service supplier. Even exercising a monopoly, as many government agencies have traditionally done, is no guarantee of continued success in such an unpredictable environment. Balancing real-time imperatives with long-term viability requires an entirely new set of stratagems.

Prerequisites for Viability

Openness to intelligence is one such stratagem. So, too, is the development of an organic capability for learning and its rapid application. Perhaps these are now the *only* prerequisites with which we need concern ourselves. If this is true, then all organizations must, at a minimum, attend to the following:

1. Meeting Derived Demands

"Derived demand" refers to goods or services (such as electricity supply, television news, or paramedic services) that are instantaneously produced and consumed. Dell's business model, for example, is based on derived demand: Your new Dell computer comes into being just two hours after it is ordered. Car manufacturers are moving this way, as are commercial fisheries and tax agencies.

Operating in real-time demands constant and active interaction with all stakeholders so that response to their derived demands can be instantaneous. If more than a few hours are needed to "link and think," you are not functioning in real time. Crucial opportunities will be missed, competitors may gain an unassailable advantage, and customers will go where their demands are better met.

2. Removing Barriers to Responsiveness

Producing to meet derived demands requires the jettisoning of many traditional organizational functions and processes that shackle or slow down your ability to remain responsive. Inventory buffers, bureaucratic distractions, overly detailed plans, annual forecasting, and inflexible approaches to budgeting or resource deployment, for example, simply get in the way.

3. Installing an Intelligence Capability

Rapid response to derived demand requires absolute reliability. But absolute reliability is dependent on your business and strategic intelligence. Knowing what is happening in the total business ecosystem of which you are a part, making sense of it, then turning this information into intelligence to change *what* you do (or *how* you do it) is critical in today's business world. So, too, is anticipating what might happen in the future and how you could respond should circumstances take you by surprise.

Consequently, establishing a robust intelligence capability entails investment in new organizational infrastructure comprising the following:

- Integrated methods for *sensing* and *making sense* of information as well as *designing* and *taking action on* appropriate strategic interventions;
- Tools like scenarios for learning about the future;
- Appropriate systems for identifying and treating strategic risk;
- Systems for distributing and optimizing new knowledge across your business; and
- Real-time audit processes and strategic performance feedback mechanisms to ensure that you are still steering toward your intended destination.

4. Reinventing the Niche

Traditionally, business models were thought to have a shelf life of around forty years. Today, because of the volatility of the connected economy (including the different risks posed by new markets, new competitors, new relationships, and new technologies) companies must devise new business models every few months. Essentially this means reinventing yourself in order to fulfil your chosen niche. The ability to remain fluid, to keep changing, embracing uncertainty, complexity, and ambiguity as autonomic routines of organizational life, now becomes indispensable for optimizing continued value creation.

5. Organizing for Dynamic Uncertainty

Capturing system-wide intelligence and using it effectively requires a highly sensitized and responsive organizational community. Furthermore, the continuous redesign and reconfiguration of the business that intelligence tends to instigate require extraordinary resilience and tolerance from your people. Highly customized work design practices, supported by appropriate technologies, will be required to build flexibility, trust, and collaboration within such a changeable environment.

These five elements, not exhaustive by any means but all responding in different ways to the need to remain *viable,* inevitably modify the strategic focus for any business.

Human beings adjust their personae and behaviors to better meet the exigencies of any situation. This is known as "adaptiveness." Adaptiveness is enabled instantly, often instinctively, through learning. In the turbulent transition from our industrial past to a networked future, organizations, too, will only survive if they are capable of rapidly adapting to varying conditions. Like human beings, organizations must learn to change as and when required in order to remain aligned within the broader social ecosystem of which they are a part. Only then can we be confident of their continuing relevance and credibility.

Living Systems

We know that viable organizations appear to behave like living organisms. In fact, the most naturally occurring viable systems are living systems. Unfortunately, living systems are extremely complex organisms, almost impenetrable in their ability to defy logic and reason. Under certain environmental conditions, however, living systems have enormous benefits over other, more conventionally structured forms of organizing, as they tend to *distribute* intelligence outward. As a consequence, living systems are more:

- *Accommodating.* They adjust to new or changed circumstances more easily;
- *Adaptive.* They shift their locus of adaptation over time from one part of the system to another in order to evolve;
- *Resilient.* Small failures and individual mistakes are relatively inconsequential, while big failures are held in check by agility in other parts of the system;
- *Boundless.* By organically extending networks beyond the bounds of their initial states, living systems build their own scaffolding to initiate further structure; and
- *Novel.* Through the exponential combinations of many individuals as well as the tolerance of individual imperfection and variation, distributed systems generate perpetual novelty.

Apart from their distributed nature, there would appear to be at least seven more critical organizing principles (illustrated in Table 2.1) underpinning viability within living systems. Principles are beneficial in that they cultivate coherence while providing a moral compass when traversing unfamiliar terrain or in rapidly changing conditions. Consequently, those principles derived from natural living systems may also point to viability within human organizations and communities, but only if we are able to transcend some entrenched beliefs concerning orthodox management practices.

Table 2.1. Principles of Viability in Living Systems and Their Implications

Organizing Principle	Implications for Viability
1. Emphasizing the nature of *systemic relationships* between an organism and its environment, ECOLOGY posits that all things, however apparently separate, are ultimately connected and must therefore affect each other (Lovelock, 1987).	You should always take into account how your decisions and interventions may affect your business ecosystem(s) because the whole system will react in some way to your actions—intended or not. A reaction may not be instant or at the most obvious location. But you can be sure that there *will be* a reaction.
2. Intimately linked to ecology, the notion of NICHE is an organism's unique status, role, and value within a broader ecosystem. Its ability to fulfill this niche directly affects its prospects for survival.	In order to fulfill its niche, your organization will need to modify and maintain its "fit" with the business ecosystem as the ecosystem itself changes over time.
3. CO-EVOLUTION refers to the reciprocity that occurs in interacting species in order for them to evolve. Biological organisms adapt to and create each other from one moment to the next, simultaneously weaving themselves into one whole system. The fundamental idea here is that of *adaptation,* specifically, the capability of the organism to adapt its niche in response to the needs of the total ecosystem.	Applying both to each individual (learning to adapt to the changing needs of the organization) as well as to the organization (as it redefines or, at times, even completely transforms itself in response to the changing needs and demands of society), co-evolution will often manifest itself as distinguishable phases in the life cycle of the organization as its identity and role mutate over time.

Table 2.1. Principles of Viability in Living Systems and Their Implications, Cont'd

Organizing Principle	Implications for Viability
4. Living systems have a way of evolving into entirely new forms that, at times, are unpredictable and therefore surprising. This is known as EMERGENCE. Some viruses, for example, appear to change how they change, making it extremely difficult for research scientists to understand their true nature. When we understand more about the dynamics of co-evolution, however, such novelty is to be expected. In other words, the fact that we encounter surprises is really no surprise.	Because emergence is essentially spontaneous and can neither be predicted nor effectively planned for, it requires special attention. You will need to establish procedures (a) to identify significant emergence as soon as it occurs and (b) to treat it should it pose a strategic risk to the enterprise or a systemic risk to the business ecosystem of which your organization is a part.
5. As far as we can tell, INTENTIONALITY is unique to human beings in that we are able to engage ourselves in a process called *consciousness*. We are able to choose a path and, by choosing the direction in which we want our lives to go, are able to bring meaning and purpose to our daily activities.	Based on the clarity of your intentions, how well you are able to share and communicate them, and the degree of coherence underlying your strategic choices, you are capable of making your organization more purposeful, more meaningful, and more "future-full" for all stakeholders.
6. AUTOPOIESIS is an important characteristic of all viable systems. It means they are able to self-organize so as to recreate their unique role continuously within the ecosystem of which they are a part.	Unlike most orthodox management systems, which impose levels of control to minimize the degree of turbulence within the system, self-organizing systems are also self-managing to the extent that they do not require (or may simply absorb) imposed authority or control so as to ensure continuing growth and adaptiveness. The World Wide Web is a fine example of this faculty to continually self-create.

Table 2.1. Principles of Viability in Living Systems and Their Implications, Cont'd

Organizing Principle	Implications for Viability
7. INTELLIGENCE is the capability developed by sentient organisms, allowing them to adapt and to co-evolve purposefully in response to perpetual novelty in their environment. Any viable system is reliant on intelligence for its very survival and adaptation.	Timely, relevant, and continuous streams of information are needed in order for us to synthesize appropriate intelligence for change and for innovation. This information, which is the lifeblood for survival in the knowledge economy, must derive from all parts of the business ecosystem (and beyond).

The following questionnaire can be used to make a rapid assessment of your organization's current levels of viability.

Viability Questionnaire

Instructions: For each question in the left-hand column, circle the letter of the response that best represents your organization.

Questions of Viability	Viability Score
1. Our role in the business ecosystem is: (a) unique; (b) impossible to determine; (c) constantly mutating; (d) paradoxical and ambiguous; (e) unknown to us at this time.	(a) = 3; (b) = 1; (c) = 5; (d) = 2; (e) = 0
2. We integrate stakeholder feedback into our planning, learning, and decision-making processes: (a) when such feedback is offered; (b) constantly; (c) when drafting the annual plan; (d) through regular surveys; (e) never.	(a) = 2; (b) = 5; (c) = 1; (d) = 4; (e) = 0
3. If we needed to rapidly reconfigure the business, we could start: (a) immediately; (b) within thirty days; (c) next week; (d) as soon as a full report had been accepted by the board; (e) none of the above.	(a) = 5; (b) = 3; (c) = 4; (d) = 2; (e) = 0

Questions of Viability	Viability Score

4. Our business environment is: (a) relatively stable; (b) uncertain yet manageable; (c) becoming more volatile; (d) totally unpredictable.

(a) = 3;
(b) = 5;
(c) = 2;
(d) = 1

5. Strategic resource allocation is undertaken: (a) on a continuous basis through the application of agreed performance criteria; (b) annually by the board; (c) quarterly by the managers in each division; (d) collaboratively as and when required.

(a) = 5;
(b) = 0;
(c) = 1;
(d) = 4

6. Our systems and processes are: (a) built for efficiency; (b) designed to be flexible; (c) engineered to last; (d) easily discarded and redesigned.

(a) = 1;
(b) = 3;
(c) = 0;
(d) = 5

7. Our people find our plans: (a) incoherent and requiring continuous justification; (b) predictable but prudent; (c) challenging but stressful; (d) authentic and engaging.

(a) = 0;
(b) = 1;
(c) = 3;
(d) = 5

8. We routinely monitor and make sense of changes in our business environment: (a) when circumstances cause us to take notice; (b) continually; (c) never (we have no need to monitor the environment); (d) at least every quarter; (e) annually.

(a) = 1;
(b) = 5;
(c) = 0;
(d) = 3;
(e) = 2

9. Our people are more often: (a) excited by our vision; (b) confused by the market; (c) finding change tough; (d) depressed and frustrated by our internal capability.

(a) = 5;
(b) = 4;
(c) = 3;
(d) = 2

10. Our strategic toolkit comprises: (a) financial forecasting and modeling; (b) computer simulation; (c) systems mapping; (d) alternative scenarios; (e) all of the above.

(a) = 1;
(b) = 2;
(c) = 3;
(d) = 4;
(e) = 5

Questions of Viability	**Viability Score**
11. Our management procedures are primarily intended to:	(a) = 5;
(a) liberate learning and wisdom across the company;	(b) = 4;
(b) encourage innovation within teams; (c) ensure production	(c) = 2;
efficiency; (d) guarantee productivity targets.	(d) = 1
12. We use control mechanisms to help us: (a) manage links and	(a) = 3;
interdependencies; (b) minimize systemic risk; (c) avoid making	(b) = 5;
mistakes; (d) understand our market alignment.	(c) = 0;
	(d) = 4

Scoring and Interpretation

After you've responded to all of the questions, go back and circle the score for your response in the right-hand column. Then total your score.

A score within the range of 51 to 60 indicates that you have a highly resilient and viable organization. A score within the range from 40 to 50 indicates that your organization is likely to remain viable as long as external conditions do not change too rapidly or unpredictably or you are not struck suddenly by an unexpected crisis. A score within the range from 25 to 39 indicates extremely low levels of viability. There is an urgent need for a more systemic and integrated approach to planning, learning. and risk management in your company. A score within the range from 5 to 24 indicates dangerously low levels of viability. In the current climate, you are unlikely to remain in business if changes are not made urgently to the way you manage and organize your company.

Organizations are frequently nonviable because their response to changing external conditions is inappropriately slow or dysfunctional. There are two key reasons for this. Both are related to information flows and intelligence making.

Inbound Information

- Intelligence is perceived too late for any effective response;
- Inappropriate information is being collected;
- Information is being distorted and filtered as it passes through the organization; and

- Relevance and connections of information to the organization are not clearly recognized or understood.

Outbound Information Control

- Instructions for action remain too complex or outside the comprehension of staff;
- Staff are too busy doing the same things they've always been doing;
- Staff are inflexible or unresponsive to change;
- Messages indicating action are distorted or diverted en route to those who will be responsible for taking action; and
- Implementing staff are not empowered to act.

These factors often produce a bewilderingly complex and expensive array of symptoms that can give rise to organizational lethargy and shock.

The solution to such problems is in raised consciousness leading to purposeful design. Organizational structures need to ensure that information pathways are able to deal quickly and effectively with all kinds of intelligence. For example, a staff member who notices something significant but does not recognize it as such could well lead to the organization as a whole missing out on major opportunities. The key is to design distributed intelligence systems that are easily accessible to all staff.

These problems of consciousness and design are better handled if we understand several important concepts:

- Significant differences between external changes and our original expectations almost always signal a need for the organization to take some kind of strategic action.
- Insightful strategic action actually comprises three sequential elements:
  - Awareness;
  - Appraisal; and
  - Action.
- Without awareness, there is often insufficient time for appraisal. And without accurate appraisal, action will often be strategically inappropriate.
- Effective, appropriate action requires practice.

Strategic Navigation

The sheer speed of change in today's business environment presents the most crucial problem for designing and implementing coherent organizational strategy. In order to be able to respond instantly (and intelligently) to changing conditions, we need to conceive of strategy not as some static, arcane, secret, and unyielding plan but as a pliable, collaborative learning process impelling the business from its present state into mutually preferable futures. In effect, strategy has become process.

A fluid, real-time approach to strategic management, however, requires new mental models regarding the purpose and role of the enterprise. It necessitates new infrastructure to liberate new thinking. And it demands that we embed intelligence, foresight, and learning into business praxis so as to be assured of sustaining innovation.

"Strategic Navigation" is one such integrated methodology. Overturning much of the conventional management wisdom of our industrial past, Strategic Navigation uses ecological metaphors (concerned primarily with learning and transformation) to balance the more familiar economic metaphors (concerned primarily with controlling and producing) habitually used by managers to this day.

By weaving together strands of intelligence about an organization's past, present, and future in the context of the business ecosystem, and by becoming more deeply conscious of how mind traps (such as the "gravitational" pull of the past) filter our perceptions of reality, Strategic Navigation focuses our attention on optimizing the whole system.

Based on the principles of living systems outlined above, it enables an enterprise to learn, grow, and remain viable in the most hostile and unpredictable of global business environments. It does this by:

- Ensuring that the design of the organization's infrastructure, management systems, and core processes fulfill viability criteria (see Table 2.1);
- Providing the means whereby individuals, work teams, and management forums are continually upgrading their intelligence in relation to the dynamics of the whole business ecosystem (including the relationships and influences between various stakeholders) and, thus, enhancing their ability to take insightful action to shape or influence these dynamics;

- Embedding new tools and practices (systems mapping tools, learning net-works, and the pervasive use of metaphor and myth, for example) whereby people can engage in strategic conversations about issues of critical importance to the future viability of the business as an integral part of their work; and

- Harnessing new technologies to link all stakeholders into a dynamic, shared community of mind.

Although Strategic Navigation refashions almost every known organizational convention, one of the more significant innovations is the manner in which Strategic Navigation uses intelligence. It is commonly recognized that, as greater numbers of critical factors change in an organization's *external* environment, so complexity increases and additional changes are required *internally* to maintain strategic "fit."

Real strategic responsiveness (acting in the moment) only becomes sustainable where strategy is a collaborative, iterative cycle of collecting and acting on critical information. It calls for the synthesis of significant patterns so that leverage points can be identified. Strategically appropriate (and systemically viable) modifications to the organization's internal capability can then be targeted, and changes can be made as rapidly as possible.

This approach is essentially improvisational in nature. It can be likened to the navigational method used to this day by Trukese seafarers who invariably set sail while responding to conditions as they arise on the spur of the moment. Utilizing information provided by the wind, waves, tide, current, fauna, stars, clouds, and the sound of the water on the side of the boat, every effort of these intrepid explor-ers is directed to doing whatever is necessary to reach their final destination.

A number of companies are discovering the advantages of navigational ap-proaches to strategic management over more resource-intensive, conventional methods. Leading-edge consulting firms, such as Business Thinking Systems, for example, rely on their capacity for continuous real-time diagnosis rather than on set-in-concrete plans or pre-packaged solutions that bear little relationship to a client's evolving issues. The Australian Taxation Office continuously monitors the global regulatory environment to ensure that new domestic tax laws are aligned with international experience. American Bruce Mau regards his Global Knowledge Design Studio as a constantly evolving ecology where the job is to deliver a com-pelling experience (see www.brucemaudesign.com). Lord John Browne (personal communication, 2000), chairman of British Petroleum (BP) and the first oilman to break ranks with the rest of the oil industry over global warming, recognizes his ethical responsibility to take BP "beyond petroleum," while Jac Nasser's notion of leaders at all levels is designed to liberate the intelligence locked up within the grass roots at Ford.

Such imaginative efforts, although deceptively groundbreaking, are usually unconnected and piecemeal (though tantalizing) applications of an emergent common sense. For the most part, such efforts lack the integrative, potent "logic" of the kind provided by Strategic Navigation. Most organizations have yet to achieve real transformation and the far-reaching benefits that will accrue from deploying methodologies such as Strategic Navigation as a whole system. The Holy Grail (of business ecosystem leadership) is still there for the taking from any company possessing the insight, will, courage, and ability to leap into the jazz-like complexity and churn of the connected economy.

Remaining Alert

Drawing on common practices in the security industry, Strategic Navigation defines four different levels of alertness conditions:

- *Condition White.* "Switched off" is where most people appear to spend most of their time. People in this condition are distracted from attending to their surroundings by their own thoughts and feelings. Furthermore, they are mentally and physically unprepared for changing events and are often startled when they finally become aware of a change, often describing it as "sudden" or "surprising."

- *Condition Yellow.* This is used as a reference point to describe a subconscious and subliminal state of awareness in which people are "switched on" to what is going on around them. By being in a high state of awareness about the environment, a part of each person's subconscious is permanently alert to dangers and opportunities. In this state, we notice important information in sufficient time to evaluate and process it. In order to shift your people from Condition White to Condition Yellow, you must:

    - "Highjack" the conversational space in your company to make it more strategic. Do this by establishing virtual chat rooms and learning networks for people to talk about world events and how trends are impacting the business.

    - Continually brief your entire staff so that they are kept informed about changes to your strategic direction and intent.

- *Condition Orange.* This is a state established by a perceived important change in the environment. This is where appraisal of information takes place. The enhanced awareness of Condition Orange buys time to evaluate information and to take appropriate and effective action. If the need for action is rapid, then a series of pre-established and practiced responses should be in place so that if an "action trigger" is detected, there is no requirement for time-consuming decision making. In order to prepare your people for Condition Orange, you must:

  - Encourage them to think in alternative scenarios. Have them play out their options in a variety of different possible futures.

  - Establish risk management simulations where those people who will need to take informed action (a) receive information from operatives, while (b) practicing designed responses to particular threats to the business.

- *Condition Red.* This mental state exists during action. It includes overall awareness, but now incorporates immediate feedback about the effectiveness of the action in the context of situational dynamics relative to the organization's aspirations. In order to ensure that your people are capable of moving from Condition Orange to Condition Red, you must:

  - Document continuity processes—sequences of actions that can be deployed immediately should a crisis impact your business.

  - Have your staff regularly rehearse and improve all continuity processes as part of your organization's risk-management system.

By "putting your organization on alert," you are ensuring that intelligence becomes a function of all those staff members who routinely interact with your organization's business environment. Their alertness:

- Improves the organization's ability to transmit useful information to more central functions (who may perceive patterns individual operators cannot); and

- Transmits control information to operatives to ensure that appropriate action is rapidly taken.

Both are vital components of viability and effectiveness.

Learning Your Way Forward

The most effective way of ensuring that your organization is sufficiently alert to changing conditions is through the pervasive use of the *ChangeBrain* strategic learning spiral. This is the principal process tool for strategic conversation, collaborative learning, and systemic development within the Strategic Navigation methodology.

The ChangeBrain spiral comprises a phased heuristic method of exploration, discovery, and critical inquiry leading to informed and insightful action. It is most effective in situations in which:

- A level of uncertainty prevails around a number of critical variables;
- There are no obvious solutions to a problem or problems;
- Patterns and trends, for whatever reasons, are difficult to establish;
- Previous experience and/or knowledge appears to be of little use;
- The degree of complexity appears overwhelming; and
- Emergent issues are creating threatening environmental conditions.

The ChangeBrain spiral is a versatile tool. While intended primarily as a collaborative "pathfinding" technology to ensure both the *active thinking* and *mindful action* of groups of people engaged in systemic development—especially where such development requires extensive "strategic conversation" around complex, uncertain, and unpredictable issues and dilemmas—this spiral can even be employed by individuals as a more immediate, personal "aide memoir" (or checklist) for unfettered thinking.

Combining rigorous analysis with intuitive synthesis, and integrating both strategic and operational intelligence from the whole system of which the participants are a part, the ChangeBrain spiral has been designed to enable those engaged in the resolution of complex issues (from individuals through work teams and whole communities) to pattern their thinking in ways that liberate the inherent wisdom within the group. Thus, use of the ChangeBrain spiral will enable you to avoid spending precious time solving the wrong problems precisely, while facilitating:

- An expanded appreciation of the broader systemic context in which any set of critical issues is located;
- Clearer, more focused perspectives on these issues;

- Greater levels of consciousness concerning the scope, dynamics, and inter-connectedness of any critical issues affecting participants and their constituency;

- The continuous use of "wideband" intelligence to help shed light on the complexity surrounding such critical issues;

- Critical inquiry to enable the injection of novelty into the thinking; and

- The mindful integration of systemic reflection into participants' thinking prior to the taking of informed action.

The ChangeBrain strategic learning spiral comprises eight phases with four transition systems (see Figure 2.1).

Figure 2.1. The Eight-Phase ChangeBrain Strategic Learning Spiral

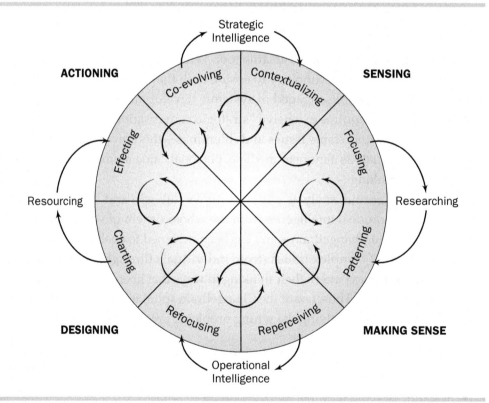

The Eight Phases of the ChangeBrain Strategic Learning Spiral

The eight phases are arranged in four linked pairs, each pair representing one type of learning domain. Although each discrete phase has its own processes and associated tools and techniques, systems arrows denote a fluidity wherein each phase can simultaneously point forward (in *development*) and backward in time (in *appraising* and *reviewing*).

At another, deeper level, the four linked pairs represent the dynamic interdependence of theory and practice. And in addressing both of these as a continuous thread through the spiral, we develop the third aspect of learning, which is learning to *become* different. In this way, the ChangeBrain process facilitates the fundamental pattern and criteria of any complex adaptive (learning) system; namely, that it:

- Acquires information about its environment;
- Acquires information about its own interaction with that environment;
- Identifies regularities in that information;
- Condenses those regularities into a model;
- Acts in the real world on the basis of that model;
- Qualifies competing models based on real-world results; and
- Upgrades its models based on real-world results.

The most subtle, and arguably significant, aspect of the model lies in its eighth phase, the precursor to moving through the next round of the spiral at a higher order of awareness. This *co-evolving* phase entails being responsive to the effects of your actions. The information that comes from these transactions are analyzed and then fed into the *contextualizing* phase as intelligence, thereby moving us into an iteration of the learning process at different learning planes, where we are able to focus on the process of learning and the nature of knowledge itself. In spiraling onto different learning planes, we are able to:

- Change what we do;
- Improve our understanding of how we are doing it;
- Reflect systemically and strategically on higher-level issues to question the value and purpose of what we are doing while simultaneously improving our understanding of it's complexity; and

- Reflect on the quality of our own thinking and thus expand our own paradigms and worldview.

Thus, the eight phases in this iterative method enable us to focus on a particular aspect of any complex issue or on sets of issues within a defined larger systemic context, where this is recognized as being based on our paradigms and worldviews at that time.

The Four Transition Systems

Each learning domain in the ChangeBrain has a product (or outputs) that acts much like a propulsion agent as it inputs into the next phase. We call these four sets of combined inputs and outputs "transition systems." These transition systems either provoke the collection and integration of useful information from a variety of sources into the ongoing process of knowledge creation or, as in the case of *resourcing,* replenish our capacity for actioning change.

The first of these, *strategic intelligence,* enables us to assess more accurately the scale, urgency, and significance of the systemic dynamics with which we are having to deal. It allows us to comprehend the scale of our predicament.

The second, *researching,* encourages us to explore certain issues in greater depth where required or to uncover what we do not know. Researching also broadens our perspectives. It confirms or challenges our assumptions and gives us direction—showing us where we ought to be looking and supplying us with more thorough information concerning the various dimensions of our business context.

As we begin to develop our ideas, the third, *operational intelligence,* ensures that we take adequate note of the more practical aspects of what is (or is not) possible, feeding us information about what we don't know that could make a significant difference in our ability to (re)focus.

Finally, *resourcing* encourages us to ensure that adequate time, skills, money, facilities, people, tools, and equipment—and particularly relevant information—are readily available to those people who will be responsible for implementing our strategy.

Using the ChangeBrain Strategic Learning Spiral

Embedded within an enterprise as the primary means for dealing with strategic issues and implementing strategic solutions in real time, the ChangeBrain spiral depicts the energy for learning and confidence for taking action required from leaders in order for an organization to remain viable over time.

Experienced as a continuous braiding of thinking and acting and navigating the waters between the past and the future, the use of this simple eight-step sequence allows us to learn how to respond to situations with far greater conviction. It also encourages us to integrate new knowledge into our capability for cognitive design. This is the level of applied learning. And applied learning allows us to act and improve our actions.

But use of the ChangeBrain spiral can do a lot more. Employing the co-evolving phase as a reflective bridge into an altogether "higher" level of learning enables us to use the entire sequence once more. This time around, however, it can be used not only to learn new actions but to learn about how we are learning to think about and "do" new actions. In this case, we can use the spiral to reflect on the very processes we've used to develop the responses we've come up with in order to address the situation at hand. This level of "meta-learning" is the level of patterning.

Finally, additional insights can be found by using the same co-evolving phase from the level of patterning as a reflective bridge into an even higher level of learning (that of learning about the nature and structure of "knowing" itself). Here, the eight-step learning sequence can be used to examine our fundamental worldviews critically. This level of learning is precisely the level we shall need to access in order to reorganize our core epistemologies, guiding principles, morals, ethics, and aesthetics.

To become so mindful is to achieve *unconscious competence.* The real value of the ChangeBrain strategic learning spiral, therefore, resides in this intrinsic development of consciousness through processes of mapping and strategic conversation. To engage in strategic conversation is to engage in collaborative learning, which is, after all, the essence of Strategic Navigation. The ChangeBrain spiral integrates multiple perspectives into our thinking, generates dialogue, and effectively maps the changing dynamics of our systems, allowing us to make more informed and insightful decisions for change. It is the continuous building of intelligence and learning from which planning and Strategic Navigation emerges.

Reference

Lovelock, J. (1987). *Gaia.* New York: Oxford University Press.

About the Author

Dr. Richard Hames *is Australia's leading business strategist and corporate philosopher. As executive chairman of the Hames Group, he works with a broad range of industry and government clients, helping them to redefine their corporate purpose, building their strategic intelligence capability, and assisting their systemic development. He is mentor to several high-profile CEOs and strategic advisor to a number of the world's most respected corporations and government agencies.*

Dr. Hames is considered an international authority on ethical business futures and was responsible for developing the Strategic Navigation methodology in conjunction with behavioral modeler Marvin Oka.

He is author of the best-selling books, The Management Myth: Exploring the Essence of Future Organizations *and* Burying the 20th Century—New Paths to New Futures.

If you would like to know more about Strategic Navigation, contact Dr. Hames by e-mail at rdhames@hamesgroup.com. U.S.-based readers are invited to call Walt Polsky at Cambridge Human Resource Group in Chicago at 1-312-251-0400.

3

Strategic Conversations in the Networked Economy

Bill Bruck

AS STAN HERMAN HAS POINTED OUT, today's economy is a networked economy. The economy is a digital economy, driven by technological change and operating under different principles from the manufacturing economy. Creating and leveraging information into knowledge assets and sound decisions is a key to business success.

"Increasingly, the value of a company is to be found not in its tangible assets, but in intangibles: people, ideas, and the strategic aggregation of key information-driven assets" (The 10 Driving Principles . . . , 2000).

In the networked economy, knowledge is increasingly created and decisions increasingly made collaboratively. People work together to pool their information and think creatively about it. Juanita Brown (*Organizational Learning at Work*, 1998) suggests that *conversation is a core business process.* I would suggest that this is because collaborative knowledge creation and decision making involve *content,* combined with *structured conversations for action.*

To add strategic value to their corporations, business leaders and the consultants who advise them must be part of the right conversations. These conversations are increasingly technology conversations: They are conversations about technology, and they are mediated by technology. An essential role for the change leader or consultant in the networked economy is to be able to participate in and facilitate these conversations. This requires two things:

1. Since organizations are increasingly global and distributed and conversations are increasingly mediated by technology, change leaders and consultants must be facile in using computer-mediated communications tools. We must be able to take the same process skills that we use face-to-face into the online realm.

2. Since a fundamental driver of the economy and organizational change is technology, and strategic conversations are increasingly permeated with technology issues, we must be conversant in the fundamental language and critical issues surrounding it to participate in those conversations.

Otherwise, we face the possibility of becoming irrelevant. Nice, helpful, and warm—but irrelevant.

Technology-Mediated Conversations

I was talking to a manager at a major telecommunications firm in the Pacific Northwest. He was looking for assistance in kicking off a virtual team initiative. I asked him how this fit into his company's overall strategic plans. He looked at me and said, "Well, it really doesn't. We never decided consciously to be a distributed organization. But what with mergers and expansions, we looked around one day and noticed that 44 percent of our employees were not co-located with their managers."

Increasingly, people who need to collaborate are not co-located. The Gartner Group estimated that "More than 80 percent of all enterprises will have at least 50 percent of their knowledge workers engaged in some form of telecommuting or other nomadic work by 2000" (Anderson & Smith, 1998).

This, plus the availability of new communications tools, has resulted in a transformation of communication within the organization and between organizations and their strategic partners.

Certain electronic tools are becoming part of the basic communications toolkit in corporate America. These include conference calls, sending and receiving e-mail with attachments, and, increasingly, electronic calendaring. Of course, reliable, always-on voice mail and fax machines are so basic that they are taken for granted.

Increasingly, companies are finding that trying to coordinate ten people's work on a common project by using e-mail is like trying to herd cats. At the same time, the range of conversations is increasing. Employees need to talk to employees in globally distributed organizations across boundaries of time, space, and departmental affiliation. Companies need to talk with and (more importantly) listen to their customers as they implement Web-based one-to-one marketing. In fact, as Christopher Locke says in the first thesis of the *Cluetrain Manifesto*, "Markets are conversations" (Locke, Levine, Searles, & Weinberger, 2000).

As a result, another set of tools is already used so much that we can predict that they will become almost as common within the next few years. These include:

- Videoconferencing;

- Instant messaging and chat;

- Online discussion forums;

- Webcasting for large groups (for example, WebEx, PlaceWare, Eloquent);

- Web-based document management (for example, Documentum's Livelink); and

- E-learning tools providing rich interactive content and peer-to-peer interaction (for example, NetG, NinthHouse, AchieveGlobal).

A third group of tools is being used now by early adopters throughout corporate America. Some will become standards; some may disappear. But change leaders and consultants should pay attention to them. These include:

- Decision support tools for brainstorming, theming, voting (for example, GroupMind Express);

- Expert knowledge sharing tools allowing people to access experts and/or resources in their organization (for example, Askme.com);

- Same-time meeting tools, which may support small and/or large groups, and include support for webcasting, application sharing, shared audio/video, and/or chat (for example, NetMeeting, Latitude, WebEx, Placeware);

- Integrated platforms for virtual teams, such as eRoom, SiteScape, Caucus, and Lotus's K-Space (these platforms provide a website where many or all the tools above are integrated into one electronic workspace, which may also include project management and workflow features); and

- Integrated platforms for communities of practice, such as Communispace or iCohere, which provide rich communications and community building tools that include many of the ones above, plus tools for quick polls, co-presence (seeing who else is online), and rich team-member profile information.

The Changing Role of Change Agents

Just like our customers, we agents of change must redefine our roles, retrain ourselves, offer new services, and create new infrastructures. Just like our clients, we need to retrain ourselves and reinvent our goals. But for many of us, this poses a problem.

Making this change will be a challenge for many OD professionals—the archetypical change agents. To be blunt, the average attendee at an Organization Development Network annual meeting does not fit the profile of a technology early adopter. Possibly this is because, traditionally, while IT (information technology) has been "from Mars," OD has been "from Venus." The approach and mentality of IT implementation has been virtually the complementary opposite to the approach and mentality of OD.

While IT professionals have been oriented toward facts, tools, and explicit specifications, OD practitioners have stressed process, people, and underlying meaning. The personality of traditional OD practitioners has been more people- than technology-centric; in fact, most OD practitioners have been somewhat *technophobic*—what Geoffrey Moore (Moore & McKenna, 1999) in *Crossing the Chasm* calls later adopters, the "show me" folks who adopt new technologies only after they are proven and their risks can be measured.

This, of course, is an attitude that we will need to struggle with in ourselves and in the profession if we are to maintain our traditional roles of diagnosing organizational problems, changing culture, and assisting in the development of teams and companies—all within an increasingly digital and rapidly changing business climate.

The good news is that change agents don't need to be "techies." *We need to be technophiles, not technologists.* It isn't important that we be able to program in Java, understand the intricacies of TCP/IP, or be able to design a corporate portal. We do, however, have to be as facile in the everyday use of technology as our clients if we are to communicate with them, and we need to be somewhat aware of leading communications technologies if we are to advise them.

Skills for Using Technology in Conversations

In the past three months, I have had the following three things happen to me in working with other external change leaders and consultants:

- When I was sending a fax, the machine rang continually. In following up with a phone call, I was told that the recipient used the same line for other purposes and I should send it again after 7:00 p.m. but call him first so he could switch it over.

- When sending a proposal, I could not send the attachment because it was too large for the AOL e-mail account the consultant had. (He also couldn't access one of the corporate websites we needed to discuss because it was incompatible with AOL.)

- I received a busy signal for two hours when calling one consultant and found later that he was on a conference call and didn't have a rollover feature because he used an answering machine rather than voice mail.

Even in 2002, situations like this happen, and it indicates that many external consultants are increasingly out of step with communications norms for corporate clients. There are new tools that our customers use to do their work, and consultants must be at the leading edge of helping them use their new tools effectively. Managers today use word processors, e-mail, and presentation software to communicate their points; spreadsheet and project management software to coordinate their work; extranets to communicate with their supply chains; and the Internet/intranet to access knowledge online. Creating documents for the Web—whether through writing html, using a web-page creation program, or merely saving Word documents as web pages—is an increasingly common skill. As PCs and the Web become the basic tools of knowledge workers, we cannot be effective as advisors—much less visionaries—if we do not share this common knowledge/skill base.

Checklist for Basic Electronic Communications Skills

- Have an always-on fax machine;
- Have always-on voice mail (so that busy signals roll over to it);
- Have an e-mail program that supports html e-mail (for example, Outlook, Outlook Express, and many others);
- Be able to reliably send and receive e-mail with attachments;
- Have an Internet connection that works reliably;
- When in the office, check your e-mail once an hour;
- If away from your desk, check voice mail immediately upon returning;
- Have an e-mail account through a business-oriented ISP (that is, not AOL);
- Use the same type of computer that your clients do if 90 percent of them use one particular type (PC or Mac); and
- Use Microsoft Office if 90 percent of your clients do (not MS Works or Word-Perfect Suite).

The list above is basic; if you'd like to be closer to the 70th percentile than the 30th, you might also consider the following:

- Get a broadband, always-on connection to the Internet;
- Sign up for one or more instant messaging services (AOL Instant Messenger, MSN Messenger), give your "handle" to colleagues and clients, and keep the service on;
- Know how to use a chat program to create a same-time meeting with two or three others; and
- Know how to use NetMeeting and start a NetMeeting session.

Of course, if you're internal rather than external, your communications tools may be mandated by your organization and you may not be able to use instant messaging, for instance. However, it's still worth understanding the tool well enough so that you could make a good argument from an OD perspective on why it should or should not be implemented in your company.

Facilitating Technology-Mediated Conversations

The use of new tools in communications has tremendous implications at a social and organizational level. Moving from voice mail to e-mail, from paper-based to electronic scheduling, or from e-mail to an online virtual team center—all of these require people to change their habits of work. They require new work flow and procedures. They often require a change management process.

That's because, at root, the fundamental principles are still valid. Virtual teams are still about teams; online collaboration is still about collaboration; and creating high-performance organizations is still about people.

As internal or external OD professionals, this change offers several opportunities. In addition to using these tools in our own communications with clients, we may be called on to:

- Facilitate meetings and other conversations that are held on these tools;

- Recommend processes for decision making that weave together use of an organization's existing tools; and

- Recommend the tools that an organization should buy or lease to enhance their communications.

In order to be able to facilitate such meetings or make such recommendations, OD professionals need to have the appropriate skills and knowledge. At the basic level, we must be able to use the more advanced communications technologies identified in the previous section, including meeting tools such as NetMeeting.

In addition to this, however, we need to learn to apply the principles of our profession in the new, online environment. Here's a checklist of several things that an OD professional might want to have a thorough understanding of in order to best facilitate technology-mediated conversations:

- How online writing is different from paper-based writing and how to repurpose documents for the Web;

- The basic principles of online business etiquette and how to get groups to agree to rules of "netiquette;"

- The principles of virtual group dynamics and their developmental stages and how they differ from those of co-located groups;

- The basic norms that distributed teams must agree on and best practices from high-performance virtual teams;

- How each form of technology-mediated conversation differs and when to use each (for example, conference calls, e-mail, chat, videoconferencing, Web-based discussions);

- How to facilitate meetings held using each type of communication;

- How to weave technology-mediated conversation tools together to create a start-to-finish process; and

- What tools a group might need in order to support the type of work the members are engaged in, which environments can best integrate these tools, and what consulting and training will be needed to implement them.

Strategic Conversations Are Technology Conversations

Every decision is a technology decision.
But also . . . no decision is a technology decision.

All right, both of these are overstatements, and they apparently contradict each other anyway. However, because of this, they can be a great meme (that is, virally propagating idea) that can help you and those you work with to keep two fundamental principles in mind:

1. In Today's Technology-Enabled Business World, Virtually Every Strategic Decision Involves Technology. Strategic decisions are those of critical importance to the enterprise: "What is our mission?" "What are the strategies for achieving it?" "What critical initiatives must be put in place?" "What is our core business and our value proposition?" Each of these is increasingly impacted by technology.

- The mission of a Bermuda tea packing company changes from local to international when it recognizes the possibilities in e-commerce.

- The strategy of using a co-located workforce on a large "campus" in a software manufacturing company changes when a company recognizes that it can have twenty-four-hour-a-day production by "following the sun" and using programmers around the world who hand off products to teams in other geographies.

- An initiative to redefine a company's mission statement, involving four hundred senior managers, can be done in three weeks from start to finish if a new online process is used.

- As an insurance company reassesses its core business, it may outsource human resources and information technology functions, since strategic partners can be tightly integrated via extranets and virtual private networks.

2. Because of Their Importance, No Decision Is Just a Technology Decision Any More. The days when an IT department could decide standards for applications with little or no meaningful input from its customers are rapidly ending. Requirements are increasingly defined by business unit owners, and IT departments are tasked with finding a way to make it happen.

Recently, for example, the IT requirement in one major player in the financial services industry was that all new applications be compatible with Netscape 4.x and Windows 95, while a two-year upgrade program was in process. Because new initiatives couldn't wait for two years, the IT director and 30 percent of the department were eventually replaced, and much of the IT process was outsourced.

Today, if the strategic requirement is that employee training be significantly upgraded and the selected solution heavily involves e-learning, and chosen vendors aren't compatible with outdated corporate standards, it's much more likely that those standards will change.

Virtually no strategic decision is merely a technology decision. The decision to purchase a custom-programmed versus off-the-shelf financial package will have implications for the corporation's ability to participate in an industry-wide electronic exchange or create a strategic partnership with a leader in an associated industry. One of the biggest mistakes that businesses can make is to leave technology decisions to the technologists.

The reason it used to be this way was that only people who talked the language of technology were the technologists. Today, while business unit owners and OD professionals may not be able to talk about *how* to implement new technology, they are much more able to talk about what the *functional requirements* of that technology must be—and that's a crucial difference.

For example, an organization may determine that it needs the following:

- Access to instant messaging through the firewall;
- Ability to use an ASP e-learning solution; and
- Ability to access corporate documents securely from a dial-in connection.

To participate in strategic conversations, OD professionals need to be able to understand some of the basic technological concepts and be able to access basic information that underlies the "what" questions—the functional requirements. In the cases above, these might include:

- What is instant messaging, and what is a firewall?
- What is an ASP solution?
- What's a dial-in connection?

What we *don't* need is the ability to intelligently converse about the "how to do it" or the technological constraints problems. For example:

- An e-learning application will overload our bandwidth, because we use an Ethernet 100 mps system and don't have redundant servers with dedicated routers and have no plans to purchase them;
- Opening the firewall will create a security problem with the x.400 protocol, and besides, instant messaging isn't a business application;
- An ASP solution means that we'd need a persistent connection through the firewall without creating an opening for hackers. We also need to determine whether port 8080 being open will cause a security problem and whether a Windows 2000 platform or SSL provides sufficient security; and
- We can't permit dial-in connections because hackers can use them to disable our systems.

These are *how* issues and they are the proper domain of the IT professionals.

In each of these cases, it's nice (although not necessary) to have some vague understanding of what the person is talking about. But what's really needed is just to be able to say, "OK, what resources will it take to solve that problem?" Or, if it's said to be impossible, the ability to find out whether other similar companies have been able to do it. Your job is to help set functional requirements.

To participate in conversations about incorporating instant messaging, you need to know *what* instant messaging is and *why* it might be useful in an organization. You need to know *how* other organizations have used it, what *best practices* have evolved, and what types of *ROI* or other benefits have accrued from it.

To participate in conversations about utilizing e-learning, you might need to be aware of what technologies are and will soon become available; how the market (customers, suppliers) will accept those technologies; and how those technologies can effectively be used to achieve various types of organizational outcomes.

Additionally, depending on your function, you might want to have some knowledge of what type of cultural change, development activities, or modifications to the organizational structure would be needed to implement a given technology initiative.

To be in the important conversations, we must be able to speak the language. The conversations that are critical to organizations today are blurs of technology and business.

Conclusion

The corporate landscape is changing. To survive, companies must change with it—as must the change agents who work with them. Increasingly, the strategic conversations within corporations are mediated via technology and involve technology issues, and we must be able to engage in these conversations to maintain credibility.

We don't need to be able to program in Java, but we need to know that it's a programming language for Web pages, that TCP/IP is used by computers to talk to each other on the Web, and what a corporate portal is. We should certainly have some good ideas about how to use a portal effectively to further strategic corporate initiatives if we want to be part of any e-business discussion.

A key opportunity for consultants and business leaders is to participate in the new conversations that are structuring the networked economy. This is ever more important, as the important conversations are a blur between the technical and organizational and "bilingual" facilitators are needed.

As we redefine ourselves as change agents for the new millennium, positioning ourselves as the conversation enablers offers us a new venue for our core competencies—to help individuals and organizations empower themselves to achieve their goals and manifest their core values.

References

Anderson, M., & Smith, C. (1998). *IEW scenario: Virtualizing the office.* Stamford, CT: Gartner Group.

Locke, C., Levine, R., Searls, D., & Weinberger, D. (2000). *The cluetrain manifesto: The end of business as usual.* Cambridge, MA: Perseus.

Moore, G., & McKenna, R. (1999). *Crossing the chasm: Marketing and selling high-tech products to mainstream customers* (2nd ed.). New York: HarperBusiness.

Organizational learning at work: Embracing the challenges of the new workplace. (1998). Waltham, MA: Pegasus.

The 10 driving principles of the new economy. . . . (2000, March). *Business 2.0.*

About the Author

Bill Bruck *is a highly respected consultant, author, and speaker in the rapidly emerging arena of use of online technology to enable virtual interaction. Because he integrates technical experience honed over two decades with his understanding of organizational systems and the people who make them work, his expertise is widely sought after by organizations deploying online work environments, e-learning, and virtual events.*

With an A.B. from Brown University, M.A. from Duquesne University, and Ph.D. in counseling psychology from the University of Florida, Dr. Bruck has been a licensed psychologist, tenured full professor of psychology, and director of institutional research at Marymount University. A prolific author, he has written ten books on human behavior and the effective use of technology. His books on Microsoft Office, WordPerfect Suite, PerfectOffice, and GroupWise have been translated into many languages and reached best-seller lists.

Dr. Bruck was the chief knowledge officer at Caucus Systems Inc. prior to joining Collaboration Architects (www.collaborationarchitects.com), where he designs electronic workspaces that support the work of distributed teams and consults in the adoption of new styles of work.

In Japanese, sensei *means teacher, and as the* technology sensei *(www.bruck.com), Dr. Bruck gives keynote presentations throughout North America on how to manage technological change using principles derived from the martial arts.*

Dr. Bruck may be contacted at the following address: 2686 Hillsman Street, Falls Church, VA 22043, phone: 703–204–8300, e-mail: bill@bruck.com.

4

Inside the
AOL Experience

Mary E. Foley

Creating Hypergrowth Results

Today we know the company as AOL Time Warner, a mega-merger of the world's largest online service and an international media giant. But just over fifteen years go in 1985, America Online (AOL) began as Quantum Computer Services with a handful of people, a fistful of money, and gripped by an idea that being online could be compelling, entertaining, and useful to John and Jane Q. Public. Seven years later, in 1992, AOL had convinced 300,000 adventurers to become online members, 150 employees to build the dream, and the SEC to grant an IPO from $38 million in revenues (America Online, 1992). By 1995, a mere three years later, the numbers soared to three million members, 1,400 employees, and $394 million in revenues (America Online, 1995). At the turn of the century those numbers continued to skyrocket. Membership exploded to over 23 million, employees numbered 15,000, and revenues expanded close to $7 billion (America Online, 2000). It's commonly considered strong economic growth in today's market for a company to achieve 10 to 15 percent revenue growth per year. But for AOL, revenues have increased by 18,400 percent and its stock value has appreciated 69,000 percent since its 1992 IPO (Stauffer, 2000). To many, AOL epitomizes "hypergrowth."

Hypergrowth essentially means growing fast—*real* fast. A temporary surge in growth is one thing. Sustaining hypergrowth over almost a decade is something altogether different. How did AOL do it? By constantly focusing on producing results—results that mattered. This focus is alive and well in the way the company operates day to day; it is at the heart of the company's culture.

How do I know? Because in the ten and one-half years I served as an AOL employee, I lived it, thrived, and felt the ceaseless demand required to play in the new economy. From 1988 to 1999, I wore several different hats, starting first as an entry-level customer service representative, progressing to mid-level training manager, then call center manager, and finally serving as AOL's first corporate training manager. AOL grew during that time from a small, hopeful start-up to a bigger-than-life worldwide brand. The company culture kept evolving, but one aspect didn't change: It's an environment totally focused on achieving results. It demands results that matter for the customer, for the growth of the business, and for the stockholders.

In today's turbulent new economy, organizations are trying to figure out the new operating rules and are feeling the pressure to produce results. Although the stock market historically abhors uncertainty, our new economic environment shows no signs of abating. Harvard Business School Professor William J. Sahlman (1999) contends that the new economy is here to stay. This strong new system, he states, "Relentlessly drives out inefficiency, forces intelligent business process reengineering, and gives customers what they want" (p. 100). Sahlman believes that in five years no part of the economy will be untouched by the pressure to decrease operational costs and reduce customer prices.

Characteristics of AOL's Results-Oriented Culture

Looking inside AOL's results-oriented culture can provide some insights and learnings for organizations reinventing themselves for the new economy. During my years at AOL, I observed and experienced seven characteristics that define the culture. Each provides a takeaway to consider for your organization.

1. Adrenaline-Inspiring Mission

2. Clear Connection

3. Customer Is King

4. Process Is Servant

5. Action Biased

6. Fail Fast, Learn, and Move On

7. Skin and More Skin

Let's look at each characteristic in more detail.

Adrenaline-Inspiring Mission

Before the merger with Time Warner, America Online's mission statement was pretty bold: to build a global medium as central to people's lives as the telephone or television . . . and even more valuable. The dominant sensation of working at AOL during its emergence was the constant feeling of excitement and belief that we were doing something meaningful. Something never done before. Many of us ran on a steady flow of adrenaline.

We believed we were making a difference. In fact, we believed we were changing the world by introducing *the* communications medium that would change people's lives forever. The most highly rated item on the employee opinion survey year after year was the belief that our individual contributions were making an impact. Having purpose included having fun, too. In March 1995, at the company's celebration of reaching two million members, CEO and Chairman Steve Case made a spur-of-the-moment challenge: He would give every employee a black AOL-etched bomber jacket if we achieved five million members within a year. We did it, Steve Case delivered on his promise, and our hearts were soaring like amateur pilots. A few years later Steve Case and COO Bob Pittman dressed as the Blues Brothers at a worldwide broadcast company meeting themed "We're on a Mission." They even had an old police car. And, of course, a blues band. Adrenaline can inspire serious fun!

With the thrill and excitement of adrenaline also comes a cost. The biggest one seemed to be that personal lives tended to get swallowed up in the spirited rush. For some, life outside the company was secondary. Personal relationships were tested and mental, emotional, and physical health challenged. Over time, murmurs of burnout surfaced as the exhaustive effects of adrenaline took their toll. Many of us were torn by the immense personal fulfillment from our careers, the financial reward it could bring, and the concessions we made to other aspects of our lives.

AOL facilitated employees' desire and ability to stay in the game by providing benefits and service to help them juggle their lives. The company offered onsite fitness centers; dry cleaning services; convenience stores with stamps, film processing, gifts, and snacks; concierge services; onsite health fairs that included many freebies such as blood screenings, flu shots, and nutrition advice; and an ergonomics program where employees could customize their workstations to relieve the physical strain of hours in front of their computers.

Takeaway: To create a results-oriented culture, an organization must generate real, adrenaline-inspiring excitement and meaning in the organization's mission. Often, the bolder, the better.

Clear Connection

It's been said that a goal is a dream with a deadline. The excitement generated by AOL's mission created intense positive energy. Employees wanted to make the mission reality. That meant clearly linking individual goals to the company's adrenaline-inspiring mission.

When AOL was small, it was much easier to understand how someone's role and goals fit into the bigger picture. This became less clear as the company grew. To enable everyone to make a clear connection and to create alignment within the company, a system for managers and individual contributors to manage day-to-day performance was created. This performance management system had two overall parts: the "what" and the "how." The "what" part intended to establish a clear connection between an individual's activities and the company's mission. Managers and their employees mutually determined what specific goals individuals should pursue in order to further the department and company mission. The "how" part provided feedback to employees on how well they demonstrated predetermined competencies and behaviors necessary to achieve these goals effectively. Not a bad design, especially given that the company's compensation system supported this view by rewarding people who got results and demonstrated the behaviors to achieve them.

In many ways, AOL's performance management system did what it was designed to do; however, several barriers prevented it from reaching its full potential. Adequate time was not spent distributing and explaining mission-generated organizational goals from senior management to middle management to individual contributors. One deterrent for senior management was that the system did not make it quick and easy to disseminate higher-level changes for people to align and realign around. There were managers who were not effective at communicating goals, which left employees to figure them out for themselves. Many did, but with risked accuracy. Middle management also found the system cumbersome to use as they tried to manage their groups' activities. Instead of the system being used as a daily management tool, it was often used sporadically or, in the worst case, as a performance evaluation form once a year.

In one senior technology manager's efforts to get everyone on the same page using the performance management system, he instituted the same five goals for everyone in his several-hundred-person department. Although the goals were legitimate, the manager did not outline what they specifically meant to each person. The manager's intent was a step in the right direction, but mass-produced goals were not enough to establish clear connection between the individual and the larger organization.

In my opinion, these are not unusual hindrances to any performance management system. However, today's technology and the latest knowledge could be applied to reduce these encumbrances. For instance, the organization could create a Web-based performance management tool immediately accessible from every desktop that states the "what" and facilitates the "how." Regarding the "what," the system would state larger organizational goals, show mapped individual goals, and describe up-to-date achievements. Alerts would instantly notify everyone of changes in organizational goals and instruct a review of personal goals for realignment. Regarding the "how," the system would describe behaviorally the competencies required to be successful in each position. Employees and managers could rate themselves, share results, and then use this as a basis for one-on-one discussion. Overall, the system would provide a common, understandable framework for clear connection with the organization and meaningful discussion and feedback on progress.

Takeaway: To create a results-oriented culture, an organization must establish clear goals that connect each individual to the organization's mission. Otherwise, at best, people will spend their time on what they believe is important, which may or may not help the organization move forward.

Customer Is King

When customers rule, they determine the results the organization creates. It's all about the customer. I remember CEO and chairman Steve Case repeatedly saying that what we do we do for our members, that we must continually listen to what they want, that we must deliver it like no one else. Attracting and retaining online adventurers was the reason AOL existed. In 1996, *Business Week* quoted Steve Case as saying, "There's nothing visionary about AOL. Its success results from simply paying better attention to what consumers want than technology-obsessed rivals do" (Cortese & Barrett, 1996). A more operational view of being customer focused came from a personal mentor who heads AOL's customer support division: "Only members print money."

Case's vision of bringing the online experience to the masses continually directed a myriad of both small and large management decisions. Some of the most strategic ones include creating an easy-to-use graphical interface, expanding service content, shifting to flat-rate pricing, integrating the Internet into the proprietary online service, and developing child safety controls.

Huge investments are made in customer support. Having spent seven years working in the company call center, it was clear to see that m*ore than half of AOL's employees are directly involved in providing free, direct support to members.* A sophisticated customer relationship management (CRM) system assists customer care consultants in solving member problems, keeps records of service problems for future improvements, and measures individual consultant performance by surveying member satisfaction after each interaction. Like the previously described dream performance management system, the CRM brings together technology and knowledge.

Customer focus in AOL's culture applies to internal customers as well. For example, during my years as part of AOL's human resources group, we were charged with enabling the company's business units to achieve their goals. We viewed ourselves as internal business partners. Each business unit was given a dedicated HR team to track with and support the unit's needs. Our goal: to minimize employee distractions and build organizational capability. Minimizing distractions meant making common HR-related transactions like enrolling for benefits, finding benefit information, receiving paychecks, enrolling for training classes, and one-on-one counseling with an HR professional convenient and easy to use. At AOL, all-but-live HR counseling was available online around the clock in every time zone. Building capability included finding, training, enabling, and retaining people to be effective and add to the organization's success.

Like external customers, what the internal customer needs and wants continues to change. During my tenure as part of AOL's human resources team, we continually reviewed and modified our activities to keep pace with those changes. When the online membership was exploding, we found new ways to recruit and select customer service reps in record time. When the company's internal hypergrowth brought hundreds of new managers with differing capabilities, we added management training courses targeted at current skills needed to operate effectively.

Continually delivering what customers want when they want it is one of the toughest aspects of putting customers in charge. AOL experienced this during what I refer to as its "connectivity crisis" of late 1996, when the company offered flat-rate pricing. Existing members loved the price change, and new customers tried the online service in droves. However, within only a few weeks, users were unable to easily get online because of system overload. Almost forty attorneys general throughout the United States were suing the company for not meeting customer demand (Stauffer, 2000). Many predicted AOL's demise. Steve Case led the comeback by publicly apologizing for the inconvenience and asking for patience while everyone in the company focused on resolving the situation. Many AOL employees, myself included, were shocked at the customer response; even *we* had underestimated how many Americans wanted to be a part of this new revolution and were just waiting for the right price to jump in. We were also embarrassed. The black leather jackets we'd proudly earned were left in the closet for fear of our being harassed, as had happened to some colleagues. Six months later, after member refunds, many Case-featured TV spot updates, and millions of dollars in phone lines and increased system capacity, customer demands were satisfied. Jackets came out of the closet. Customers were still in charge, and they knew it.

Takeaway: To create a results-oriented culture, an organization must continually focus on what customers—internal and external—want and need. That means having a relationship with your customers, the more direct the better. That means having systems and ways to continually capture customer needs and reactions. That means delivering what customers want faster and better than anyone else.

And that means admitting mistakes early and making up for them as swiftly as possible.

Process Is Servant

In a results-oriented culture, structured processes or procedures must enable results or be eliminated. There is no time for "red tape" or bureaucracy or anything that doesn't help get things done in today's fast-paced environment. I remember COO Bob Pittman saying more than once that AOL wasn't a company of process, it was a company of results.

Making process or procedures a slave to customer results is simple to understand; it's not so simple to do. What some consider a reasonable amount of process, others think include unnecessary steps. Also, when procedures are in place, they can be difficult to dismantle or change.

AOL valued its entrepreneurial environment from the very beginning. Since any process was strongly associated with needless bureaucracy, prescribing specific ways of doing things was resisted. However, people's views were more open to what I call "reasonable infrastructure" after they had experienced mounting frustration over inefficiencies associated with the company's hypergrowth. Despite that, implementing effective procedures required the strong, vocal support of senior management, or else the procedures were simply ignored.

The process created for "green lighting," or approval of projects, is a great example. When AOL was small, it was fairly easy to choose initiatives, understand roles, keep coordinated, and make decisions. In the late 1980s and early 1990s, when AOL first made a name for itself in the Macintosh community, there were only a handful of Mac developers and business development folks onboard. I served as a trainer for customer service representatives. When I needed to find out about the upcoming version enhancements for my training classes, I'd simply trot down the hall and poke my head into the lead developer's office. He'd show me what he was currently working on (and how cool it was) and explain what to expect in the next release; adding new features seemed fairly straightforward.

As the company grew, such simple enhancements were no longer simple. Functional responsibilities were dispersed to departments often separated by divisions and geography. Confusion and frustrations escalated, since no formal process existed. Work got done, but with increasing pain. A formal green-lighting process was finally put in place. Service enhancement ideas would now be pitched to a cross-functional group who approved or rejected them. The project could only be fully approved after a thorough marketing requirements document was created and reviewed. This was not a complicated process, but one that enabled the end result. Still, as one colleague close to the dilemma put it, implementing even that level of process was like giving birth, and it never would have happened without full participation from senior leadership.

Keeping process secondary to customers hasn't always been easy for AOL. By its very nature, technology and engineering-related work is very flow-chart oriented and process driven. Much of the technology needed to deliver the online service wasn't available in the early 1990s; AOL had to create it. Once the core technology was built, more focus could be put on adding more services for customers. "We really don't care about the technology. We've tried to recognize it as a means to an end, and the end is to improve the way people get information and communicate," Case told *Time* magazine in 1997 (Ramo, 1997). Technical folks had to start sharing power with the service content folks. Not easy. Suddenly, the technical mindset of structure and process was viewed as less important and sometimes a hindrance to the creative service mentality. Although riddled with potential conflict, this dynamic tension served the customer by providing the best of both worlds.

Takeaway: To create a results-oriented culture, an organization must be good at using process and procedure wisely. Not process for process' sake, but process that enables results or is eliminated.

Action Biased

The essence of being action biased is the preference of action over inaction. Perfect action is not the goal; movement in the right direction is. Presenting an idea or issue "partially baked" is usually good enough to determine whether it's headed toward the desired result. If you attempt to polish the idea before presenting it, you've lost precious time, a much greater sin in today's new economy. We often joked when I was at AOL that we were flying at 20,000 feet while building the airplane. But we were taking action and believed we were headed in the right direction.

Every project, every effort I ever worked on at AOL had aggressive timelines. Working in that environment "corrupted" me; I naively believed all of corporate America worked that way. I realized otherwise when I began working with third-party vendors and found myself measuring their ability to deliver a quick response. The organizations I chose to work with were those that delivered quality with a sense of urgency. When, for instance, I spoke with a major training and consulting firm about developing leadership training, they delivered a customized program within four weeks. Another firm was able to create from scratch an online employee survey capability within a few months. Both organizations continued to keep pace and we enjoyed successful partnerships.

Ironically, with all this bias for action, sometimes AOL got stuck in indecision. Be it lack of information needed, lack of clear ownership, or lack of urgency, occasionally decisions were slow to move forward. For example, one large cross-departmental project was to "build or buy" a server for the advertising group. After many debates, time-consuming data-gathering efforts, and much confusion, the project's senior technology manager grew impatient and made an executive decision to build the system internally and be done with it. And so it was. Some say that if someone hadn't made such a definitive decision, the company would still be without that server today.

A significant corollary to AOL's action bias is that it didn't matter much who you were if you could get the job done. Even organizational rank was less important. People cared much more that you knew what you knew and that you could apply it effectively and quickly.

This corollary is particularly significant to me, since I was offered several opportunities based on my performance and potential rather than age, gender, or experience. At age 29, I was charged with leading and tripling our technical call center to 250 employees. The majority of my staff was male and many of them older than I, but together we produced results and created incredible morale. The company got what they wanted . . . and so did I. This corollary seemed, however, to break down at the senior level. Although Steve Case sought individuals with strong capabilities that complemented his strengths, mitigated his weaknesses, and focused on results, few women or minorities held top-ranking positions. Movement in that direction is one bias for action I would personally support.

Takeaway: To create a results-oriented culture, organizations must possess a bias for action and make decisions quickly. It doesn't matter who you are as much as it matters that you can get the job done.

Fail Fast, Learn, and Move On

In the action-biased, frenetic environment of today's economy, some decisions don't turn out to be the best ones. When that happens, quickly regroup and re-choose. Take the stake out and replant it. Sometimes a change in customer need or another unforeseeable factor causes a completely different decision and direction. Sometimes only an adjustment is required. Other times, it was not the right decision at all. There is no time for huge egos in a results-oriented culture. Resiliency and tenacity are much more valuable.

Many considered AOL's previously mentioned connectivity crisis the consequence of flawed decision making. Surely, the public thought, AOL must have known the pent-up customer demand. Instead of making excuses, the company quickly and publicly admitted the problem and took action to fix it. Marketing was suspended, members were offered refunds, millions were spent to increase system capacity, and TV ads featuring Steve Case were aired to keep the public informed of progress. AOL had failed fast and big and took swift action to change direction—proof that mistakes don't have to be devastating.

An area where many believe AOL should have responded more quickly is in dealing with "spamming," those e-mails that rudely invade mailboxes with lures and advertisements, often sexual in nature. Millions of AOL members created new fertile ground for these e-mail marketing wannabes. Amidst fuzzy legislation and AOL's reluctance to act as "big brother," many members felt seriously harassed. Not only is spamming invasive, it eats up valuable system capacity. Eventually AOL took legal action against the offenders and continues to develop ways to block the critters from entering. Unfortunately, however, like the hardy cockroach, these bugs keep finding new ways to enter member accounts. Many wished the exterminator had arrived sooner.

What's interesting about AOL's growth and rise to power is that it happened despite its mistakes. In 1996 alone, the company racked up enough problems to put any company at risk: a connectivity crisis, a highly publicized dismissal of a new COO, a system shutdown for nineteen hours, and a change in a marketing accounting practice that wiped out much of its previously stated profits. But how is a company to avoid errors when it's forging new territory? It can't. It must instead have a strong "fail fast, learn, and move on" perspective. I like how David Stauffer (2000) puts it in *It's a Wired, Wired, World: Business the AOL Way*: "The AOL experience, then, confirms the advisability of, first, barreling full speed ahead for continuing growth and innovation, being prepared for unavoidable miscues, and expressing genuine regret and determination to make things better when mistakes are made" (p. 176).

Takeaway: To create a results-oriented culture, an organization must be willing to fail fast, quickly admit mistakes, learn from them, and redirect to move on.

Skin and More Skin

We hear of more and more companies these days offering employees equity in their organization. The idea is that, if employees are part owners, they will stay longer, work harder, and be more concerned about doing things that make the company successful. For start-ups, it can also provide an attractive alternative to the high cost of salaries. Immediate needs for cash are offset by the potential for greater individual gain in the future.

AOL offered employees "skin in the game" before this idea became so popular. New employees received stock options as part of their new-hire package. And not just senior managers, everyone: individual contributors and managers, full-time and part-time. In addition, the company's compensation system annually offered more skin by rewarding ongoing results. There was no automatic cost-of-living or other such increase, only salary increases and more stock options based on performance. I like to think of it as "no results, no rewards, no apologies."

One drawback of rewarding employees so heavily on individual results is that it sometimes works against creating team results. More and more work is accomplished through project teams. Teaming well is essential to getting projects done well and quickly. AOL could improve its reward system by measuring and rewarding team results in addition to individual results. The suggested performance management system could be expanded to capture project evaluations from both the project manager and participants. The "what" section could include the project's goal and whether the goal was met. Individual contributions could be recorded, but team results would be rewarded. The "how" part would capture project manager and participant evaluations based on teaming related behaviors.

Takeaway: To create a results-oriented culture, an organization's compensation system must provide real skin in the game to all players and reward results. You get what you measure and pay for.

Ambiguous Results or Results in Ambiguity?

In today's new economy there is no other real choice but to be results-oriented. Information technology has dramatically increased the speed of work and reduced operational costs. Globalization has opened more markets and created more competitors. Wall Street expects consistent profit and growth. The rapid pace of change has significantly reduced any company's ability to predict or control future events accurately. This combination of performance expectations and reduced predictability compels companies to focus on performing now as they monitor and respond to emerging events. Ambiguity is the norm. A results-oriented culture can provide context and clarity to effectively make things happen in the midst of ambiguity.

AOL: A Hypergrowth Anomaly?

Yes and no. AOL's tenacious ability to produce results and grow so rapidly has been truly amazing. Few companies in the last decade can compare. However, the company culture enabling these results is not entirely unique. Research studies and commentary about highly successful companies reveal some of the same characteristics. Collins and Porras' (1997) *Built to Last,* for example, underscores the power of a compelling mission. Still, there's something unique about AOL's internal environment: *intensity.* The seven characteristics used to describe AOL's results-oriented culture didn't come from an analysis of business literature or a management consultant model. They came from my deep impression of being there. Ten and one-half years can leave lots of impressions. The biggest: Every day was intense; every day we were there to make things happen. The characteristics of AOL's results-oriented culture aren't as revolutionary as the relentless implementation of them.

Getting a Clue
Some Provocative Questions for Discovering Just How Results-Oriented Your Organization Is

Here are some simple, thoughtful questions to ask yourself and others to discover just how results-oriented your organization is. Think of these questions as a guide to probe into common organizational behaviors that may have advancing or undermining effects.

Adrenaline-Inspiring Mission

1. Does the organization's mission statement have an emotional component that plucks at your heartstrings, or is it just a plaque on the wall provoking the common response, "Yeah, right. . ."?

2. Do people work late or go the extra mile to show their company commitment more than at other places you've worked? Are people excited about what they're doing? Are you?

Clear Connection

1. Do people know the company's goals for this quarter or this year? Do you?

2. Can people easily state their current projects or goals and how they fit into a bigger company picture? Can you?

3. Is it clear how your position helps the company? Would you create this position if you owned the company?

4. Do you know when the company's overall goals change, or do you feel left in the dark?

Customer Is King

1. Do organizational leaders talk much about customers? What they want? How the organization is responding?

2. Does the company behave as though it has to compete for customers?

3. Can most people easily name their external or internal customers? Can you?

Process Is Servant

1. Are there lots of processes and procedures? Do they stifle getting things done, or do they create order out of chaos?

2. In your role, have you ever tried to put some kind of process into place? Did you experience any resistance?

3. Have you ever seen a procedure changed or process eliminated in this organization? Was it a big deal?

Action Biased

1. How common is it to have lots of meetings where nothing really gets done and no real decisions are made?

2. How much approval is usually needed to start a project or implement an idea? Are there several management layers, or is one enough? What happens if someone goes ahead and then seeks approval later?

3. Do people have to pay their dues before moving up, or are they given opportunities because they're effective?

Fail Fast, Learn, and Move On

1. Is your company trying to come up with new products, services, or ways of doing things to stay competitive? Does this feel messy? Do you feel the company is making overall progress?

2. Can you think of company events where major decisions were made and then redirected or retracted? How well do you think this was handled? Was the customer reaction positive or negative?

3. How important is saving face around here? How comfortable are you with making a risky decision? How about your colleagues?

Skin and More Skin

1. Do people share in the company's financial success beyond salary and annual increases?

2. What are increases based on? Producing results? Certain behaviors? Specific skills? Cost of living?

3. Does senior management believe that employees should have some kind of equity (for example, stock options) in the company? Do you feel they believe people are the key to the company's success, or do they mainly talk about revenues and other numbers?

References

America Online. (1992). *AOL's annual report.* Dulles, VA: Author.

America Online. (1995). *AOL's annual report.* Dulles, VA: Author.

America Online. (2000). *AOL's annual report.* Dulles, VA: Author.

Collins, J.C., & Porras, J.I. (1997). *Built to last.* New York: HarperBusiness.

Cortese, A., & Barrett, A. (1996, April 15). The online world of Steve Case. *Business Week.*

Ramo, J.C. (1997, September 22). How AOL lost the battles but won the war. *Time.*

Sahlman, W.A. (1999, November/December). The new economy is stronger than you think. *Harvard Business Review,* pp. 99–106.

Stauffer, D. (2000). *It's a wired, wired world: Business the AOL way.* Milford, CT: Capstone.

About the Author

At age 33, **Mary E. Foley** *retired independently wealthy from America Online, where she started ten years earlier as an $8 per hour customer service representative. During those years, she learned that being bodacious rather than a "good girl" was the only way to thrive in the new economy. In her new book,* Bodacious! An AOL Insider Cracks the Code of Outrageous Success for Women *(AMACOM, 2001), which is co-authored with Martha Finney, she shares strategies to achieve personal and career success in today's constantly changing environment.*

Currently, Ms. Foley shares her gutsy, strategic message as an author, speaker, and life visionary through her company Bodacious! Ventures, LLC (gobodacious.com). In addition, she serves on the board of HumanR, a human resources software and consulting company, for which she is an angel investor. Parts of her story have appeared in Kiplinger's Personal Finance, Fast Company, *and* Across the Board *magazines. She holds a B.S. in industrial engineering from Virginia Tech and an M.S. in organization development from Pepperdine University.*

Part 3
Collaborative Challenges

HOW **DOES THE NETWORKED ECONOMY** affect the way people work together? This section focuses on the virtual teams imperative, examining the fundamentals of virtual teams and illustrating some of the practical realities of installing and developing virtual teams with an actual case.

In Part 3, the authors concentrate on the tactical level with actual cases and models of virtual teaming, as well as a detailed description of the uses of information technology integrated with behavioral science for large-scale systems change.

In Chapter 5, Jeremy Lurey reports on the critical success factors for virtual teams and their implications for improving team effectiveness. Among other points, he concludes that "Virtual team leaders must select only those individuals who are qualified to perform virtual work" and describes the criteria that apply. He also emphasizes that team members must focus on developing supportive team member relations and establish positive team processes early on. This is a point with which Carol Willett agrees in her presentation in Chapter 6 of an actual case involving many, perhaps most, of the typical issues that confront change leaders as they try to transition from longstanding traditional assumptions and attitudes into the challenging new requirements of networked organizations.

In describing their "Whole System Transformation Conference" in Chapter 7, Roland Sullivan, Linda Fairburn, and Bill Rothwell provide a model and information technology tools for speeding up the rate of large-scale organization change.

5

Virtual
Teamwork

Jeremy S. Lurey

AS THE MARKETPLACE CONTINUES TO CHANGE, many of today's largest corporations are evaluating whether or not they are ready to compete in the new economy. Faced with the need to be more agile and respond to the market more quickly, these companies have recently been questioning the way in which their businesses are structured. Based on the results of these analyses, a number of companies are realizing the urgent need to redesign their corporate structures to meet the demands of this ever-changing marketplace.

The increased pressures of these emerging market conditions, then, have brought resurgence in corporate transformation and restructuring. The growing trends of mergers and acquisitions, e-commerce, and especially globalization have created this need to implement more flexible and versatile work arrangements.

Organizations focused on achieving business goals such as speed, cost, quality, and innovation are now turning to virtual teams (groups of individuals working on shared tasks while distributed across space, time, and/or organizational boundaries) to sustain their business advantage. Some examples of this include the following:

- A management consulting firm that can utilize the specialized talents of globally dispersed business consultants to complete their client deliverables much faster by working twenty-four-hour shifts around the world;

- A high-tech firm that can significantly enhance product distribution by connecting technical engineers and marketing experts spread across international operations during the development process; and

- An agricultural firm that can increase sales and overall revenues by maintaining and sharing consistent information with sales representatives who work all across the United States.

As these examples suggest, the use of virtual teams is becoming more and more prevalent in today's business environment because of the added value these teams provide. To achieve these benefits with virtual teams, however, we must first identify what factors lead to success when working in a virtual world and then understand their impact on our virtual efforts.

Critical Success Factors for Virtual Teams

While many believe that virtual team effectiveness is entirely dependent on the technical tools a team is equipped with, there are actually several factors that impact the performance of a virtual team. These variables relate not only to the available technologies but also to the social makeup, geographic dispersion, and the primary objectives of the team. As a result, virtual team leaders might focus on designing a supportive atmosphere that manages these traits rather than on spending their precious resources simply trying to implement the "perfect" technical environment to enable their teams.

While different virtual teams may require slightly different solutions, five specific factors have proven to play a critical role in establishing the foundation for success, according to empirical research conducted by the author as well as personal experiences while working with and consulting to virtual teams. These critical success factors are depicted in Figure 5.1.

Figure 5.1. Five Critical Success Factors for Virtual Team Effectiveness

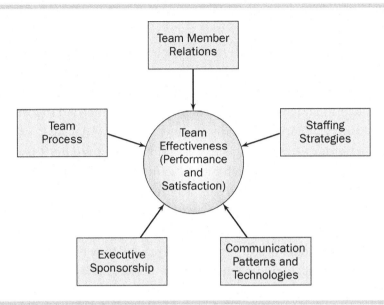

Source: Jeremy S. Lurey. *Five Key Strategies to Improving Your Virtual Teams.* Presented at International Conference for Advances in Management, Baton Rouge, LA, July 1999.

Strong Team Member Relations

Strong team member relations rooted in a well-nurtured sense of interdependence must exist for a virtual team to be effective. Creating this relationship of mutual dependence begins as quickly as team members experience a sense of shared purpose. Having all team members share their understanding of the team's mission and discuss any initial questions or concerns creates the necessary environment for collaboration to occur. Resolving these simple misunderstandings in the beginning is surely easier than stumbling over potential conflicts that might develop later on. Clarifying the team's mission and overall business strategy, then, is critical to begin the bonding process among team members.

Providing individual team members the opportunity to meet each other early in the team's development and to interact socially can be extremely helpful in expediting this process. In fact, team leaders should take full advantage of any time spent together by scheduling adequate time for interactive team-building activities. In this face-to-face environment, team members can get to know one another better and develop personal relationships. In-person meetings will not deliver these expected benefits if they are completely focused on handling business-related issues.

Two researchers who are well-versed in virtual team operations sustain this view. In their popular book, *Virtual Teams,* Jessica Lipnack and Jeffrey Stamps (1997) state that "group formation was difficult across distances using electronic media alone. The integrating degree of psychological closeness needed to form the group was aided strongly by face-to-face discussions" (p. 140). They also write, "Virtual teams have a harder time getting started and holding together than collocated teams. Thus, they need to be much more intentional about creating face-to-face meetings that nourish the natural rhythms of team life" (p. 140).

Interdependence, however, cannot exist among team members if they do not learn to trust one another. Virtual teammates must rely on one another to provide both technical and emotional support. For this reason, they must pay special attention to building trust during each phase of work. Having this trust becomes increasingly important because of the added pressures team members experience when coordinating work tasks and trying to maintain productive relationships at a distance.

Charles Handy (1995), an author who reinforces the imperative for trust in virtual organizations, writes, "Trust is the heart of the matter. That seems obvious and trite, yet most of our organizations tend to be arranged on the assumption that people cannot be trusted or relied on, even in tiny matters. If we are to enjoy the efficiencies and other benefits of the virtual organization, we will have to rediscover how to run organizations based more on trust than on control" (p. 44).

In his work, Larry Meeker (1996) also discusses the need to have trust in a virtual team environment and refers to it as a key enabler. He writes, "For teams, it is vital to have effective relationships among team members—relationships that are based on trust. When this exists, the team finds success in areas such as communication, timely decision making, successful problem solving, and cooperation between team members. When trust is absent, negative emotions and actions . . . can detract from a team's productive energy, and undermine and bankrupt the positive work the team should be attending to" (p. 267).

Developing strong team member relations, then, occurs when team members have a shared sense of interdependence and trust one another. A useful strategy for building trust is to create space for team members to get to know one another. Whenever possible, this space should include a face-to-face meeting where individuals can interact more easily and connect with one another on a personal level. Although face-to-face meetings can be challenging due to the required coordination and potential costs involved, it is the most basic tool for gaining commitment for the virtual effort at the beginning and perhaps the most effective way to ensure high performance in later stages of team life.

When in-person meetings cannot be arranged, sharing personal information and concerns electronically can also expedite the bonding process among dispersed teammates. At the beginning of a project, team members should be encouraged to ask questions about the team's overall purpose or clarify their individual roles on the team. In addition, understanding individual work styles can greatly improve the working relations among team members. Depending on the team's access to certain technologies, these conversations may take place via group telephone conference, videoconference, or even through e-mail. Creating a team roster that includes personal photographs in addition to individual contact information can also help personalize the relationships among distant team members.

Building trust, however, takes time. People develop trust in one another by working together and learning that they can depend on one another. Another important factor in building trust involves learning to understand and appreciate differences among people. Individuals who have not previously worked together need to be reassured that their new teammates are reliable. In a virtual world, this process can be expedited by establishing simple policies and group norms that highlight how work will be performed. Emphasizing timelines for completing work tasks or setting guidelines for regular team communications provides a basic framework and creates clear expectations for everyone. Team members who meet these shared expectations from the start demonstrate that they can be trusted.

Positive Team Processes

In his book, *Groups That Work (and Those That Don't)*, Richard Hackman (1990) acknowledges that some teams experience positive outcomes simply by achieving success early on in their development. He writes, "Groups that somehow got onto a good track tended to perform even better as time passed, while those that got into difficulty found that their problems compounded over time" (p. 481). One explanation for this trend comes from the design process used when initially building the team.

The ultimate goal of the design process is to create a team that is capable of performing the tasks required by the organization. This process, then, requires an assessment of the team's objectives. If the team does not understand its goals, it will experience tremendous difficulty in performing its work. Developing the team's mission is also critical to the team's success. Without this understanding, individuals will not have the sense of purpose needed to be able to commit to the team effort.

Several structural issues, like team type and composition, need to be addressed during the design process as well. Team leaders need to specify whether the team will consist of individuals from one department or will be cross-functional, whether it will disband after completing its assignment or will continue intact as a more permanent work team, and so on. After these structural elements are confirmed, the new team members must be identified. This is especially important in a virtual team because it takes a unique person to be able to work at a distance, and oftentimes in isolation, from one's fellow team members. Selected individuals must possess all of the knowledge and skills required to achieve the team's objectives. Due to the increased dependence on information technology in the virtual team setting, team members must be able to communicate electronically through the available tools and perform their work with little supervision or technical support as well. To ensure that team members are capable of performing their work, some training may be required to develop individual skills and team capabilities prior to activating the team.

After securing the team's purpose and internal membership, the team's external relations with the larger organization require focused attention. Ideally, the team will be designed in such a way that it is self-managing, but the team must maintain its connection to the rest of the organization. The team leader, therefore, must support the team and facilitate its process whenever necessary. One principal area of responsibility is providing access to company resources. These resources might include data files, special equipment, or other necessary materials. Given the team's virtual design, this may require outfitting the team with additional tools or technologies, as well as granting user privileges to information that would otherwise be secured.

During this design process, there are two common setbacks that teams often encounter. First, many teams are unable to utilize the specialized knowledge and competencies that exist within the team's membership. By failing to recognize the skills or poorly managing them, less effective teams are forced to operate with limited information and limited perspectives. Second, teams tend to be less effective when they have difficulty reaching a shared understanding about what team members are trying to accomplish or how to achieve these goals.

Virtual teams already contend with the challenges of working at a distance and cannot afford to be set back by these common obstacles. To avoid these roadblocks and get on the fast track for success, several conditions must be met. First, all team members must believe that the team can be effective in achieving its goals. In addition, team members must share the workload to minimize any social loafing that would otherwise occur. Furthermore, good communication and cooperation within the team must be present. In fact, this is especially true in the case of virtual teams where team members need a clear protocol detailing how to communicate with fellow team members.

For example, e-mail can be an effective tool for sharing information with distributed teammates, but when is it more appropriate to hold an electronic conference? E-mail is useful for sending brief status updates or file attachments that need to be reviewed by others. Conducting a brainstorming session via e-mail would be extremely challenging though, since the communication does not occur in real time. Technologies like group telephone or videoconferencing, on the other hand, would be much more effective. The meeting would be easier to coordinate and more productive if team members could participate in an open dialogue and share their ideas in a real-time forum. E-mail, however, may be the only available means for enabling this exchange if team members are confronted with language barriers or are spread across multiple time zones and cannot come together at the same time.

In the dispersed workplace, virtual teams must also follow through on their early successes by establishing formal team processes. Scheduling progress reviews at periodic intervals is one important team practice. These activities help team members regularly assess their work and quickly redirect their efforts when needed. Establishing standard issue tracking and resolution procedures also drive effective team operations. In addition to helping the team monitor its progress, these procedures mitigate potential conflict before it arises by reinforcing a focus on the team's objectives and not on personal differences.

Another critical team process that must be addressed is decision making. While it is important to have a leader, all team members should be involved in the decision-making process. If individuals are not encouraged to participate in the process, then they may perceive decisions to be arbitrary and thus will be less likely to support them. Moreover, team members may not feel their ideas are valued if decisions are made without consulting them. This can be extremely damaging in a virtual team since team members often work in isolation and need to be honored for their contributions.

Virtual teams should also take time out to mark the completion of significant milestones. Bringing team members together for team celebrations can be a great method for recognizing team accomplishment. These gatherings also go a long way toward reinforcing team-member relations and energizing the team prior to launching the next phase of work.

A high-tech team involved in the research and development of new software products used this strategy very successfully. This team consisted of team members who worked across the United States and Europe. The U.S. contingent focused primarily on marketing and distribution of the new products, while most of the actual development took place in France. Because of the logistics in conducting their work, team members were rarely co-located and thus depended on advanced technologies to maintain contact. Whenever they finished major work streams though, the team members would get together in a mutually agreed on location—sometimes at the wineries in Napa Valley, California, and other times at the beaches in the South of France—to celebrate their recent success and plan the next phase of work. These team events created a safe environment for discussing lessons learned during the prior effort, while also enabling productive conversations about improving the process for future work.

When face-to-face events are not feasible, virtual teams should still hold electronic conferences to celebrate their work. These meetings can still create the needed space to review what worked well in completing previous tasks and what efforts can be improved in the future. This form of debriefing is especially valuable when individuals are typically focused on their immediate work tasks and rarely step back to consider the bigger picture. When the debriefing is over, team members should also discuss their plans for completing the next set of tasks. Developing this roadmap will help keep them focused during the next phase of work.

Effective Staffing Strategies

Distrust, technophobia, resistance to change, and inaptitude for ambiguity are common personal traits that make it difficult for certain people to function in a virtual world. For this reason, only certain people will be able to perform, let alone find satisfaction from, virtual work. Therefore, selecting the right people to be part of the team is essential.

In their book, *Globalwork,* Mary O'Hara-Devereaux and Robert Johansen (1994) describe some of the key characteristics needed for individuals to enjoy working in geographically dispersed virtual teams. They claim that one basic requirement is "a high tolerance for ambiguity. Technical competence is certainly important, but most of the challenges do not have purely technical solutions. For the most part, both the challenges and the qualities needed to succeed are to be found in the human personality" (p. 106). Based on her experience with virtual teams, Beverly Geber (1995) also recommends that team leaders should "select people who are comfortable sharing information and working with computers, but also make sure they're people with strong personalities who can assert themselves in the electronic medium" (p. 39).

These are important factors to consider when selecting team members, because those with strong personalities in face-to-face settings may not project such a dominant presence in a virtual setting. This is often attributed to an unfamiliarity with the technologies and can be overcome with experience. However, it might also be related to a deeper inability to command attention in an electronic medium where the nonverbal cues are severely limited. At the same time, identifying individuals who can effectively communicate their ideas in an electronic medium may be challenging, since people who appear to be shy or introverted in person may be the most valuable virtual team members. Clearly, a delicate balance of communication skills and technical abilities is needed so that virtual team members are not only comfortable expressing their ideas with others but also capable of doing so with the tools available to them.

Effective virtual teamwork demands the presence of these team players; thus, the chances of fielding a successful team are greatly improved if team members are chosen carefully. Team members should not be selected simply because they are available or are not succeeding at their current tasks. Virtual team members, instead, should be identified based on their existing skills and capacity to adapt to, and even thrive in, a dispersed work environment. Furthermore, people who require minimal supervision and direction are preferable, as they will likely prove more successful in a distributed work group. Matching the right people to these virtual roles, then, is imperative to enhance performance in a virtual world.

Team leaders might do best to use both formal and informal methods to identify potential candidates for emerging virtual teams. Most organizations utilize formal channels to post open positions and allow their employees to pursue the opportunities if they are interested. If team leaders have been successful in communicating the virtual team's mission and objectives, especially in relation to the overall business strategy, then employees will be intrinsically motivated to join the team.

In addition to this formal mechanism, virtual team leaders can also contact individuals directly if they fit the profile for virtual work. Some of the traits to look for include strong communication and technical skills, ability to work well with others, initiative in seeking increased job responsibilities, satisfaction with challenging environments, and history of high performance ratings on previous assignments. These individuals are usually pretty easy to locate within the organization, but team leaders might not be able to simply remove them from their current responsibilities, especially if their current managers do not understand the purpose of the team. Intervention from a person of authority may be required to negotiate a compromise in this situation. For example, the top performer may serve as a part-time resource to the new team, or he or she might accept the new assignment for only a short period of time. Depending on the situation, any number of arrangements can be considered.

Supportive Executive Sponsorship

In a team-based organization, executive leadership takes on new meaning. The style of command-and-control management that once dominated traditional hierarchical companies does not work in this complex work environment. Methodologies based on the principles of micromanagement and authoritarian supervision do not contribute to building trust over distances. Virtual teams, therefore, need their executive sponsors to facilitate their process by stating the objectives clearly and providing general guidelines for the approach. They do not need them to define the exact process the team will use.

Executive sponsors will be effective only when they inspire virtual team members through a clear vision and communicate a sense of enthusiasm for the change. The new role of an executive, then, is to guide and support the team, not drive it in one particular direction. In their book entitled *Teams & Technology,* Mankin, Cohen, and Bikson (1996) write that leadership in this technology-driven team-based environment "is more akin to group therapy. The leader asks the right questions, reassures the team members that they are on the right track, and helps them deal with tension and anxiety" (p. 106). In this regard, successful virtual teams rely on their executive sponsors to connect them to the corporate vision and business objectives, not regulate how they conduct their work.

This style of facilitation and coaching requires the executive sponsor to possess several key skills. First, the sponsor must have the ability to coordinate teamwork across geographical and cultural boundaries. This process generally requires the executive to specify the team's mission and clarify any miscommunications. At the same time, this person must be willing to relinquish authoritative control to those who are conducting the work. In fact, effective virtual teams can often be measured by the extent to which team members perform their own internal task management. The executive sponsor, however, is still ultimately responsible for the team's success and must recognize the need to intervene when the team is not achieving the stated objectives.

In addition to facilitating the team's processes, these executives serve as the team's champion to the surrounding organization. In this role, these sponsors must be completely dedicated to supporting the team and promoting its best interests to all stakeholders. They must position the virtual operation as a key business initiative and gain the support of any leaders who might otherwise impact the team's ability to achieve its objectives. Without this visible sponsorship, others may not understand, and thus not approve, important requests from the team.

If executive sponsors are fully engaged in the process, then there is no question as to the importance of the team's work. Any leader will understand the critical need to dedicate appropriate resources to the team and will do so whenever needed. Depending on the situation, this might require increased budgetary funding, more powerful information technologies, team member training sessions, or even additional team members. Regardless, the executive sponsor must promote the virtual effort and ensure that dispersed team members have all of the necessary tools for performing their work tasks.

Finally, these sponsors play strategic roles in helping virtual team members utilize the technologies that support their work. Consequently, these executives must excel in communication skills and be technically competent with all forms of electronic communication to support their dispersed teams. Successful virtual team sponsors, then, serve as positive role models and present the right message for using these technologies, just as they expect their team members to do the same.

Formal Communication Patterns and Advanced Technologies

Although these processes and strategies can be extremely helpful in promoting team effectiveness, virtual teams are only capable of performing their work if they are equipped with the proper tools. In a distributed setting, the importance of information systems increases exponentially because space and/or time separate most team members. In fact, the virtual work environment would not exist without the most recent advances in technology systems. The current technologies, then, can be credited for creating the electronic connections between dispersed individuals.

For a virtual team, all of the latest communication and information technologies constitute the required toolkit. This arsenal consists of all the common tools, such as telephones, fax machines, voice mail, and e-mail, which we often take for granted in today's standard workplace. In addition, remaining connected to our dispersed teammates requires more advanced technologies, such as group telephone and videoconferencing, shared databases, and groupware applications, which many of us use less frequently.

When working across distances, having a shared understanding of how to use the technology is often just as important as having the technology—the technology, in and of itself, is not enough. Virtual team members need a clear understanding of what technology to use and when. Given the availability of multiple communication channels in this electronic environment, team leaders must develop a protocol for proper, and consistent, usage patterns.

When selecting the most appropriate communication vehicle, understanding the primary functionality, strengths, and weaknesses of each of the available tools can be extremely useful. The following table contains some basic information to consider when evaluating possible communication and information technologies (see Table 5.1).

Table 5.1. Recommended Tools and Technologies by Team Application

Tools and Technologies	Team Application
E-Mail	For brief to moderate exchanges of information, including the transfer of electronic documents
	Strengths: Ability to distribute unique personal messages and/or group messages asynchronously via text; able to archive exchange for future reference; can be very cost-effective compared to other alternatives
	Weakness: Difficult to maintain long exchanges, especially among multiple participants
	Common Uses: Distribute status updates to the entire team or send documents to team members for review and feedback

Table 5.1. Recommended Tools and Technologies by Team Application, Cont'd

Tools and Technologies	Team Application
Voice Mail	For one-way delivery of small bits and pieces of information
	Strength: Ability to distribute unique personal messages and/or broadcast messages asynchronously via voice
	Weakness: Difficult to have any dialogue; difficult to capture and archive history
	Common Uses: Give a quick "heads up" without having to interrupt fellow team members
Personal Telephone Call	To share ideas or discuss important information in a live conversation with a single team member
	Strength: Ability to have an involved two-way dialogue in real time; real-time connection promotes strong team member relations
	Weaknesses: Both participants must be available at the same time; cannot archive conversation; no visual images or cues
	Common Uses: Discuss performance issues and talk through potential solutions
Group Telephone Conference	To share ideas or discuss important information in a live forum with all team members
	Strength: Ability to conduct an involved group conversation and create dialogue in real time; real-time connection supports informal team building
	Weaknesses: All participants must be available at the same time; meeting can be significantly impaired by language barriers or poor facilitation; cannot archive conversation; no visual images or cues
	Common Uses: Review status and raise any new issues or concerns
Video Conference	To share ideas or discuss important information in a live forum with all team members
	Strength: Ability to conduct an involved group conversation and create dialogue in real time with visual images and cues

Table 5.1. Recommended Tools and Technologies by Team Application, Cont'd

Tools and Technologies	Team Application
Video Conference, cont'd	*Weaknesses*: All participants must be available at the same time; meeting can be significantly impaired by language barriers, technology problems, or poor facilitation
	Common Uses: Conduct strategic planning sessions; celebrate team success
Face-to-Face Meetings	To share ideas or discuss important information in a live forum with all team members
	Strength: Ability to conduct an involved group conversation and create dialogue in person in real time, including all verbal and visual cues
	Weakness: All participants must be located in the same place at the same time; can be costly due to associated travel and facility requirements
	Common Uses: Conduct brainstorming or strategic planning sessions; celebrate team success
Fax	For immediate exchange of printed information
	Strength: Ability to send and receive hard-copy materials quickly, especially documents that require signed authorization
	Weakness: Any modifications to the text must be re-entered in electronic versions; extremely difficult to capture history
	Common Uses: Forward contracts and other time-sensitive materials; send documents for review
Standard/Express Mail Delivery	For routine exchange of printed information
	Strengths: Ability to transfer large documents and any materials requiring original signatures; supports color and black-and-white printouts
	Weakness: Can take several days or even weeks for delivery
	Common Uses: Forward legal documents; deliver final results or presentations

Table 5.1. Recommended Tools and Technologies by Team Application, Cont'd

Tools and Technologies	Team Application
Shared Databases/Groupware	For ongoing exchange of information, especially electronic documents
	Strength: Ability to develop central repository for creating, storing, and recalling information as needed; ability to capture history for future reference
	Weakness: Technical infrastructure and access to shared information required for all team members
	Common Uses: Archive draft work products as well as final deliverables

To illustrate this point, consider a common situation that one virtual team experienced. This virtual leadership team consisted of several managers who represented five regional sales teams of an agricultural firm in the United States. This team, charged with coordinating the activities of the five regional teams, conducted status meetings every other week to discuss sales forecasts and share product information. The team's communication challenge was that they all traveled extensively and rarely had access to advanced technologies such as Internet connections or videoconferencing at the time of their meetings. For this reason, the team selected group telephone conferencing and e-mail to facilitate their sessions. Team members distributed the meeting agenda and other materials to be discussed via e-mail the day prior to the meeting, and then they participated in the live discussion and reviewed this information together during the conference calls. The advantage of using these tools was that they were cost-effective and they met the lowest common denominator of available technologies.

In addition to these common tools, groupware, workflow, and document management technologies are also required to help virtual teams manage their electronic data. The key challenge that results from the convergence of these communication and information technologies is how to create, share, and reuse knowledge without being subjected to information overload. For this reason, advanced communication and information technologies do not themselves create an effective virtual team, but they remain one of the necessary components to maintain real-time communications and achieve success in the virtual world.

With a clear understanding of the factors that most significantly impact virtual team effectiveness, taking stock of a team's operations can be extremely beneficial. Regularly evaluating performance throughout the team's life is imperative to minimize any misguided efforts and steer the team back on course. The questionnaire below can be used to assess the functioning of a virtual team in relation to the five factors for success (see Exhibit 5.1). Depending on the results of this assessment, a variety of interventions might be needed to redirect the team and enable a continued path of success.

Exhibit 5.1. Questionnaire for Benchmarking Virtual Teams

The following survey provides fifteen key questions to ask in order to benchmark a virtual team's performance against the five factors for success.

- ☐ Are team members selected for the team based on their individual talents and abilities?

- ☐ Are team members technically competent in using the available tools and technologies?

- ☐ Does the executive sponsor communicate the vision to team members and the surrounding organization?

- ☐ Do team members have a shared understanding of the team's purpose and overall business objectives?

- ☐ Do team members trust each other to perform quality work in a timely manner?

- ☐ Do team members maintain contact with one another on a regular basis?

- ☐ Does the team successfully use a complement of tools and technologies to exchange routine business information (that is, phone, telephone/videoconference, e-mail, shared databases, face-to-face, and other means)?

- ☐ Do executive sponsors promote the use of electronic communication and information technologies?

- ☐ Does the management approach promote team member participation in decision making and issue resolution?

- ☐ Is time dedicated to conducting team-building activities and further developing team member relations throughout the life of the team?

Exhibit 5.1. Questionnaire for Benchmarking Virtual Teams, Cont'd

☐ Do team members hold team celebrations and plan future phases of work at the completion of major milestones?

☐ Does the team complete its work on time and within budget?

☐ Is the team effective in reaching its goals and stated objectives?

☐ Does the team function like a cohesive unit?

☐ Do team members enjoy being a part of the team?

The Importance of Executive Sponsorship

On further analysis of the causal relationships between these critical success factors, an interesting pattern emerges. Although each factor affects at least one of the other variables, executive sponsorship demonstrates the greatest impact on the other variables (see Figure 5.2.).

Figure 5.2. Causal Relationships Between Executive Sponsorship and Other Critical Success Factors

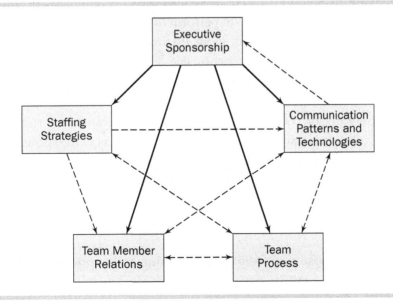

Source: Jeremy S. Lurey. *Five Key Strategies to Improving Your Virtual Teams.* Presented at International Conference for Advances in Management, Baton Rouge, LA, July 1999.

With the help of the right executive sponsor, a virtual team can receive the full support of the entire organization. On the other hand, a virtual team that is not backed by the right sponsor might never receive the vital resources needed to be successful. For this reason, executive sponsorship provides the best entry point for designing a strategy to enhance virtual team performance. Any action plan to improve the effectiveness of a virtual team must therefore begin with securing dependable executive sponsorship.

As previously noted, executive sponsors perform two critical functions. First, they establish clear expectations and guidelines for their virtual teams. Second, they establish the necessary environment and provide the required resources to meet the stated objectives. These sponsors must then empower their teams to be self-sufficient and trust them to perform the work. At the same time, they must be quick enough to recognize when team members are struggling and provide more direct supervision or additional resources if they cannot manage the work on their own.

Given the increased pressures of the new economy, virtual team members must focus on performing their work. They cannot afford to spend their time lobbying for more money or advanced tools. If dispersed team members need to conduct a design session in person, the sponsor must endorse the meeting and approve the travel schedules and budgets for everyone. If virtual teammates are struggling to maintain communication with one another, the sponsor must recognize the need for additional team training and/or more integrated technologies. In some cases, the executive sponsor may be able to perform these actions without seeking additional approval. On the other hand, there are times when the executive must consult with and gain approval from other business leaders. For this reason, executive sponsorship is critical for a virtual team to obtain the right resources.

Given the severe requirements that are placed on these executive sponsors, one might ask how a person could ever perform all these functions. Unfortunately, there is no simple solution because it depends on the conditions of the specific situation. The style of leadership one enacts must accommodate a number of factors, including the cultural conditions, geographic distribution, available technologies, and operational mission unique to the team. Because every team is dynamic and constantly evolving, sponsors must decide which method is best, given their own circumstances.

Consequently, those responsible for designing and supporting virtual teams might choose to concentrate their efforts on creating conditions that will truly enhance team performance. Instead of micromanaging group behaviors, effective executive sponsors will devote their energies to developing situations that increase the likelihood of team success. Some of these conditions include appointing only the most qualified candidates to the team, explaining the team's purpose and over-all business objectives, clearly defining individual team member responsibilities, and providing team members access to the information and tools they need to get the job done. With this structure in place, sponsors can still leave ample room for individual team members to implement their own approaches and techniques to manage the work. The checklist in Exhibit 5.2 provided below highlights some of the most important activities for designing a supportive environment that promotes virtual team effectiveness.

Exhibit 5.2. Checklist for Designing and Supporting Virtual Teams

The following checklist identifies the top fifteen activities virtual team members and their leaders must perform to create and maintain the right environment for their virtual teams to succeed.

☐ Consider organizational imperatives and define business case for implementing virtual teams.

☐ Clearly articulate vision and corporate objectives to all employees.

☐ Design virtual jobs that are challenging and intrinsically rewarding.

☐ Select team members based on individual talents and abilities, including technical competence and interpersonal skills.

☐ Explain team purpose, roles, and responsibilities to all team members.

☐ Conduct initial face-to-face meeting to clarify team objectives and facilitate team-building activities.

☐ Establish processes for sharing information, making decisions, and resolving miscommunications or potential conflicts.

☐ Ensure that team members have clear goals and recommend potential approaches to perform work.

☐ Equip team with required communication and information technologies.

☐ Provide team members access to all information needed to perform work tasks.

Exhibit 5.2. Checklist for Designing and Supporting Virtual Teams, Cont'd

☐ Demonstrate use of electronic media through ongoing team communications and group conferences.

☐ Facilitate technical workshops and interpersonal training sessions to help team members work in dispersed environment.

☐ Encourage stronger interpersonal relationships through trust and respect for team members.

☐ Promote initiative by including all team members in important team activities.

☐ Recognize individual and team efforts through rewards and other performance incentives, such as team celebrations.

At its core, the executive sponsorship function depends on the leader's abilities as well as on those of the individual team members. Executives need to develop positive team processes and encourage their team members by involving them in traditional management activities. For example, the executive sponsor and individual team members must work together to define work parameters, including reasonable objectives, project timelines, and communication protocols for maintaining regular contact and conducting "virtual check-ins." The team members are then responsible for structuring their own work environment and monitoring daily performance. At the same time, the sponsor can assume a supervisory role and simply keep apprised of the team's activities through scheduled status updates or requests for additional guidance. By enacting strategies that increase team member participation in these processes, executive sponsors shift some of the responsibility to the team members and encourage them to take ownership over their own fate.

Domestic Versus Transnational Virtual Teams

Although this set of best practices is applicable to all types of virtual teams, empirical research conducted by this author (see Lurey, 2000; Lurey and Raisinghani, 2001) suggests that there are slight differences between teams that are dispersed across domestic and those across national boundaries. Whether they work in a specific region or across the United States, members of domestic virtual teams often perform their work with less difficulty. These individuals share a common culture and language that helps them interact with one another. They may not see one another in person very frequently, but they are still able to understand one another and react as needed.

The most critical success factors for domestic teams, then, are based on defining clear roles and procedures as well as establishing a sense of trust among team members. These teams most commonly rely on e-mail, personal telephone calls, and voice mail to maintain contact with one another. They also use fax and group telephone conference technologies, standard and express mail delivery services, and face-to-face interactions to exchange business information. In many virtual organizations, they do not utilize videoconference technologies, because they are unable to achieve the same quality of interaction experienced during in-person meetings. Given the technical and quality issues related to holding videoconferences, it is sometimes more practical for domestic virtual teams to meet face-to-face.

When working across national boundaries, however, several issues become more prevalent and can significantly impact the team's performance. Unlike their domestic counterparts, members of transnational teams bring several different cultures and languages to the team. This diversity may be beneficial in the long run, but it can create tremendous barriers early in the team's development. The varied experiences and broad perspectives team members have often create confusion if team members do not define the primary purpose of the team and are not clear about their objectives. For this reason, it is imperative for transnational virtual teams to establish even more formalized processes and even stronger interpersonal relationships.

In addition to these common success factors, these teams are heavily dependent on their internal team leaders to facilitate routine interactions and monitor their work progress. These leaders must develop clear procedures for problem solving, decision making, and conflict resolution. If needed, they can also recommend new ideas or approaches to clarify how best to perform the work. In essence, internal team leaders serve to keep the team working together by supporting ongoing communications and work activities.

Like their domestic counterparts, transnational virtual teams also rely on e-mail, personal telephone calls, and voice mail to conduct routine business. Due to the difference in geographic distance and time zones, as well as the increased associated costs, these teams do not utilize fax and group telephone conference technologies, nor do they use standard or express mail delivery service as often as domestic virtual teams do. Instead, they utilize shared databases, groupware, and other technologies such as Internet chats more regularly to exchange business information. Transnational teams also hold videoconferences to maintain contact and simulate face-to-face interactions more frequently than domestic teams.

Implications for Improving Virtual Team Effectiveness

While there are clear differences in how virtual teams are arranged as well as in how they perform their work, the true essence of a virtual team is not so different from that of a traditional co-located team. Virtual teams are still dependent on all of the same variables that affect the functioning of regular teams. Although the tools and methods can be significantly different, any efforts to improve the effectiveness of a virtual team must be based on the same activities that one would initiate with a co-located team.

Virtual teams, however, require added connectivity to overcome the vast distances that separate team members. Toward this end, more formal processes and communication protocols should be developed. First, the individual team members' roles and the team's primary objectives must be explicit, not simply assumed, due to the physical distances that separate team members. Without a crystal-clear understanding of their goals, "the progress of [team] members will be stymied," reports one virtual team member who regularly interacts with colleagues across the United States to provide litigation support to his corporate clients.

Furthermore, strategies specific to virtual teaming must address the need for more personal contact among team members. In fact, one member of a transnational research and development team believes, "Knowing someone on a face-to-face level and creating relationships with them through social interactions outside of work really helps each individual understand the strengths throughout a team."

For these reasons, organizational leaders who try to improve the performance of their virtual teams by simply providing them with more advanced technologies may be misdirecting their resources. These sophisticated technologies are essential and play an important role in establishing the basis for a virtual teaming effort. The internal dynamics and team processes, however, are also critical to achieving success in a virtual environment.

Conclusions

Virtual teams may soon become the primary operating units needed to achieve a competitive advantage in today's global marketplace. An increase in corporate restructuring has created the need to design more flexible and versatile work arrangements. Given the increased competition of the new economy, organizations are focused on achieving business goals such as speed, cost, quality, and innovation. The inaccessibility of critical resources, especially information, has prevented even the most well-designed organizational teams from accomplishing their objectives.

Virtual teams may face significant challenges in performing their work remotely; however, communication and information technologies are enabling such work relationships and helping them overcome more traditional barriers. Teams of dispersed individuals, even those that cross national boundaries, now obtain critical information and complete their tasks more efficiently. With the right technologies, anyone can connect to any piece of information, regardless of where that person is physically located or where the information actually resides.

Technology alone, however, does not guarantee effective virtual team performance. Executive sponsors play a pivotal role in either supporting or inhibiting the abilities of their virtual teams. If these leaders focus their efforts on developing formal processes and procedures, building strong interpersonal relations, and encouraging effective communications, their virtual teams will be more successful in conducting their work. For this reason, team sponsors must attend to their teams' internal dynamics as well as their organizational surroundings.

References

Armstrong, D.J., & Cole, P. (1995). Managing distances and differences in geographically distributed work groups. In S.E. Jackson & M.N. Ruderman (Eds.), *Diversity in work teams: Research paradigms for a changing workplace* (pp. 187–215). Washington, DC: American Psychological Association.

Geber, B. (1995). Virtual teams. *Training, 32*(4), 36–40.

Hackman, J.R. (Ed.). (1990). *Groups that work (and those that don't): Creating conditions for effective teamwork.* San Francisco: Jossey-Bass.

Handy, C. (1995). Trust and the virtual organization. *Harvard Business Review, 73*(3), 40–50.

Huber, G.P. (1990). A theory of the effects of advanced information technology on organizational design, intelligence, and decision making. *Academy of Management Review, 15*(1), 47–71.

Lipnack, J., & Stamps, J. (1997). *Virtual teams: Reaching across space, time, and organizations with technology.* New York: John Wiley & Sons.

Lurey, J.S. (1998). *A study of best practices in designing and supporting effective virtual teams.* Doctoral dissertation. California School of Professional Psychology, Los Angeles.

Lurey, J.S. (1999, July). Five key strategies to improving your virtual teams. In *International conference for advances in management conference proceedings.* Baton Rouge, LA.

Lurey, J.S. (2000, May). Best practices for domestic and transnational virtual teams. *Symposium on Individual, Team, and Organizational Effectiveness Conference Proceedings*, Denton, TX.

Lurey, J.S., & Raisinghani, M.S. (2001). An empirical study of best practices in virtual teams. *Information and Management, 38*, 523–544.

Mankin, D., Cohen, S.G., & Bikson, T.K. (1996). *Teams & technology: Fulfilling the promise of the new organization.* Boston: Harvard Business School Press.

Meeker, L. (1996). Trust: The great team enabler. In G.M. Parker (Ed.), *Handbook of best practices for teams, volume I* (pp. 267–272). Amherst, MA: HRD Press.

Nunamaker, J.F., Dennis, A.R., Valacich, J.S., & Vogel, D.R. (1991). Information technology for negotiating groups: Generating options for mutual gain. *Management Science, 37*, 1325–1346.

O'Hara-Devereaux, M., & Johansen, R. (1994). *Globalwork: Bridging distance, culture, and time.* San Francisco: Jossey-Bass.

About the Author

Jeremy S. Lurey, Ph.D., *a principal at Plus Delta Consulting, specializes in assisting client organizations, ranging from small start-ups to some of the world's largest corporations, manage the transitions related to systems implementation, process improvement, corporate restructuring, and strategic planning efforts. He has extensive experience working with executives and managers in conducting organizational assessments, designing change strategies, facilitating leadership development, enhancing team performance, and implementing performance improvements.*

Dr. Lurey earned his Ph.D. in organizational psychology after completing his dissertation, A Study of Best Practices in Designing and Supporting Effective Virtual Teams, *an applied investigation of several domestic and transnational virtual teams. He has since authored numerous articles on virtual teaming and e-learning techniques and frequently presents at professional conferences and seminars on these topics.*

6

Ready for Virtuality
A Case

Carol Willett

What Is a Virtual Team?

Do virtual teams bring to mind 3D-visored and electronically gloved technophiles melding minds in cyberspace? The reality is both more prosaic and more complicated. To say that a virtual team is a group of people who use computer networks as their primary mode of interaction, communication, and collaboration is an accurate but not particularly helpful definition. This is because we have two nebulous and often misused terms in play—"virtual" and "team."

A *team* is a relatively small number of people working collaboratively, who share purpose, performance goals, and an approach for which they hold themselves mutually accountable. Because team efforts blend both individual results and collaborative work products, the output of the team is greater than the sum of the parts. A *work group,* by contrast, is a group of people working independently of one another to produce a collective product. Work group members are individually responsible for accomplishing specific tasks. The output of a work group is equal to the sum of its parts. The distinction is an important one because in geographically, organizationally, or substantively diverse and dispersed teams, the issue of performance expectations and mutual accountability is critical to team success.

"Virtual" is another term that is subject to loose usage. Teams become *virtual* not simply by dint of the technology they use to communicate, coordinate, and collaborate, but because the automatic default option of meeting face-to-face no longer works as their primary mode of interaction. Teams may discover the need to work virtually because their members are scattered over many different organizational boundaries. They may be separated by geography or time zones. Or they may belong to wholly different professional communities. Whatever the necessity that prompts a team to learn to collaborate via technology, an indispensable facet of its success will be the extent to which team members can make explicit their tacit assumptions about the following:

- What it means to be a part of this team;
- What roles and responsibilities are involved;
- What participation level is expected; and
- What behaviors are "in bounds" and what behaviors are "out of bounds."

A Case in Point: Teams at DOE

Let's begin by looking at a fairly typical, traditional quality team process at the Department of Energy (DOE). As we trace its evolution from face-to-face work group to virtual team, it becomes clear why negotiating performance expectations is a critical aspect of virtual team success.

Quality Circles to the Rescue

During the 1980s, DOE's Office of Security and Safeguards embraced the Quality Circle approach as a means to improve its regulatory and policy process. The goal was to enhance the safe handling of our nation's nuclear materials. Several hundred volunteers were recruited or appointed from throughout the DOE national system of laboratories, power plants, production plants, and project offices to take part in the policy review process. They represented a mix of professions as well as a range of sometimes conflicting organizational equities and interests. Their mandate was to review policy as drafted by DOE Headquarters in order to surface any inconsistencies or exceptions based on local situations and to anticipate what would be required to effectively implement these policies.

What the Old Process Looked Like

DOE Headquarters led and controlled the process by sending hard copy drafts through the U.S. mail, then soliciting, collating, and integrating the results in a sequential editing process that looked something like a tennis match. This iterative, sequential, back-and-forth editing process was supplemented by phone calls and e-mail. The process from first draft to issuance sometimes took a year or more to complete. When there were particularly contentious issues to be resolved, DOE would host periodic conferences for Quality Circle members to meet and thrash out their differences face-to-face.

After a decade of this process, DOE was spending several million dollars a year to bring Quality Circle members from geographically distant locations to a series of week long conferences. The process was slow, cumbersome, and had become prohibitively expensive. Quality Circle participation (both in the conferences and in subsequent coordination via snail mail) was unpredictable, since Circle service was not seen as a core job responsibility.

Circle Member Reactions

The Circle members themselves were frequently dissatisfied with the process, complaining that they never really knew what other Circle members were contributing, nor did they understand the relationship between their input and ultimate policy decisions. Field offices accused DOE Headquarters of being arbitrary in their decisions and unresponsive to requests. Headquarters felt the Circle participants were overly parochial in their views and sometimes uncooperative.

Barriers to Effectiveness

Several barriers stood in the way of the Quality Circles becoming teams—much less virtual teams.

Lack of Cultural Readiness. For the most part, Circle members did not see themselves as members of a team. If anything, they saw themselves as the designated defenders of their site's interests against the machinations of other DOE sites pursuing their own suspect agendas. Members belonged to autonomous organizational elements and were not mutually accountable. There was little if any experience in teams that crossed organizational boundaries within DOE. The norm in DOE had been that knowledge and information moved vertically between DOE Headquarters and the local sites; it did not move laterally across site boundaries in the normal course of things.

This lack of cultural readiness is not unusual for virtual teams. Teams whose configuration is that of a planet made up of large numbers of co-located people with just a few geographically dispersed members (think of them as moons) invariably experience a tug of war over access to information and decision-making forums and a struggle over identity.

Lack of Social Readiness. Other than those who shared a job title or specific functional responsibility, members saw little point in collaborating with people from other parts of the DOE community. Due to past differences of opinion, interest, and experience, some Circle members were very reluctant to work with other members. Efforts at face-to-face collaboration in the past had, in some cases, been exceptionally difficult. Most virtual team members want to know, "Who are these other people?" "What are they good at?" and "What's in it for me if I agree to work with them?" An essential prerequisite for effective collaboration is the sort of relationship building that answers these basic questions.

Lack of Appropriate Communication and Collaboration Tools. That most basic mechanism of sharing tacit knowledge—a reliable telephone directory—did not exist. It was difficult for Circle members to initiate or sustain a dialogue because there was no easy way for one expert to identify or contact a counterpart unless they had previously met face-to-face. Nor were there easily accessed electronic reference libraries. Policy archives existed in hard copy at Headquarters and were mailed out as requested by field elements. There was no one place where Circle members or the larger DOE population could scan a composite reference library online.

Lack of a Shared Collaborative Technology Platform. DOE had no system-wide intranet. Each site had its own hardware and software systems, entrenched IT interests, and independent budgets for technology support. Word processing applications and software versions varied widely from one site to another, and Circle members frequently found it impossible to read one another's e-mail attachments. It was literally (as well as figuratively) impossible for Circle members at some sites to talk with one another, other than through extended rounds of telephone tag.

So What Drove the Change?

Along with the rest of the federal government, in the past five years DOE has felt the pinch of significantly reduced budgets. Because of the proven value of Quality Circle input in the past, DOE was unwilling to dispense with the Circles altogether, but it needed to find a way to gather and integrate their input at a substantially reduced cost—both in terms of travel dollars and time and level of effort. In collaboration with an external consulting group, the Office of Security and Safeguards decided to experiment with eight of its more than twenty different Quality Circles. The question was, "If we give them the technical tools to work virtually, will they do so?"

Negotiating the Cost of Admission

Given the social history of some of the Circles and the negative experience of many Circle members with DOE-sponsored technology in general, Circle members were not wildly enthusiastic about the prospect of being trained as virtual teams. Workshop leaders decided to address this head on and asked three provocative questions:

1. What are your pet peeves about serving as a member of a team (any team)?

2. What are the drawbacks of serving as a member of this team (the Quality Circle)?

3. What are your reservations or concerns about being asked to become part of a virtual team using technology to do its business?

Circle members were voluble about the lack of individual recognition, lack of accountability, and lack of leadership that they felt had characterized other DOE teams of which they had been a part.

Members were surprised to find that they shared many of the same complaints about being a member of this particular Circle—the inability to know what other people were doing, the difficulty in determining the impact of individual contributions, and the seeming impossibility of coming up with an easy, convenient, and timely way of working out differences other than through annual face-to-face conferences.

Their reservations and concerns about learning to work together virtually included the following:

- Anticipated time required away from current responsibilities ("There's no way my boss is going to understand me spending a lot of time on the Internet when I've got real live fires in my in-basket");

- Opportunity costs ("My plate is already full. How do you expect me to accomplish this too?");

- The prospect of working with difficult people who don't know as much as I do about the subject at hand ("Why should I spend time sharing knowledge with people who can't help me in return?");

- Boss's expectations and reluctance to cede control ("Look, my boss doesn't want anything to go out of our site unless he's seen it first, and now you're telling me that I'm supposed to collaborate with people he doesn't know exist?"); and

- Aggravation factor in learning to use new technology ("This is too hard—at least with paper and pencil I know I won't make a mistake." "You're asking me to learn yet another system?!?").

After venting all these concerns, Circle members were a little breathless as the workshop leaders asked them, "OK, given all this, what would make it worthwhile to you to be able to work virtually?" People broke into small groups to discuss three questions:

1. What payoff in my day-to-day work do I need to see for this to become something I value?

2. What information, knowledge, and contacts would I like to have at my electronic fingertips that would make my work (including my Circle responsibilities) easier?

3. What behavior do I expect to see from my fellow Circle members in order for this team to succeed?

What followed was a fascinating process of how people in virtual teams negotiate their performance expectations of themselves, of each other, and of the team as a whole.

Getting Clear on the Payoffs

Initially, Circle members focused only on the policy coordination process itself, stating that "It would be nice if policy review took less time," "I'd like to be able to see what other people are saying," and "I want to minimize the amount of travel involved in making sure we have policies we can live with."

After a few minutes of reviewing the collaborative tools and going through the team workspace, members began to brainstorm other possibilities that would make these changes to the work process worthwhile:

- "How about if we could have the policy references online so we would know what was current?"

- "I'd like some sort of an online functional directory so that I could identify my counterparts at other sites without having to memorize twenty-six different wiring diagrams."

- "What I really need is some way to reach people quickly rather than our current process of telephone tag."

Discovering the Information Resources of the Group

The discussion on payoffs led into a broader consideration of not only the information that everyone wanted to have at his or her electronic fingertips but the information, expertise, and knowledge resident within the team itself. At first, the group focused on all the information "at Headquarters," which people wanted to be able to directly access online. Within a few minutes, however, Circle members were beginning to say things like, "You know, I've got a training program model on that. Do you want to see it?" "Maybe those of us who have to deal with this all the time could write down a few of the things that work (and don't work)," and "What if we had some way to put templates or models in a shared library so that we're not always having to create everything from scratch?" In this somewhat circuitous way, members began to explore the assets and resources they each brought to the team beyond their functional responsibility as site representatives to the Circle.

As the workshop facilitators posted all the contributions to the collective "wish list" of the group, individuals began to warm up to the idea that there were benefits to be had in moving from their previous, individualistic approach to that of a collaborative, mutually accountable (if virtual) team.

Negotiating Performance Expectations

With these tempting possibilities dangling before them, Circle members were then asked to brainstorm ways to complete the sentence, "You know you're on an effective team when . . ."

The responses on five densely written flip charts fell into these overall themes:

1. *People Respect Confidentiality.* Given the diversity of organizational cultures, agendas, and priorities represented within the Circle, members felt it was essential that everyone agree to abide by and to respect rules of confidentiality during Circle discussion of policy. The last thing anyone wanted to have to worry about was that a frank discussion of the difficulties encountered in implementing policy would "leak" to higher echelons before the Circle itself had discussed and resolved their differences. This was universally agreed to be the "kiss of death" for the team.

2. *Members Respond to Each Other.* A second important issue was defining reasonable time limits for response—to e-mail, to phone calls, to pages, to requests for assistance from within the collaborative website—on issues central to the Circle. This discussion pointed up how widely Circle members differed in their work schedules, travel commitments, and use of technology. The only thing all members agreed on was that they all had too much to do given the amount of time available. For that reason, all standards for responsiveness were measured against the question, "Under normal conditions, can I respond within these limits most of the time?" The team also agreed that in those cases in which members could not meet the identified response times for "priority" requests, they would make a best-faith effort to communicate when they could respond.

3. *Contributions Are Acknowledged.* A longstanding complaint of Circle members was that they never knew whether their input had been received, had made a difference, or the reasons why it was not incorporated into policy. A condition of team participation was that members wanted to hear from Headquarters, and from each other, an acknowledgment of their efforts and contributions. As one gentleman poignantly put it, "In thirty-five years here, I have yet to hear anyone say, 'thank you.'" The team was clear that if the performance expectation of members was that they would make timely and comprehensive input on policy, they wanted timely and clear feedback on what had been done with their input and the impact as a result.

Lessons Learned in Negotiating Performance Expectations

The following lessons emerged from the negotiation process among eight separate virtual Quality Circles:

1. It's the relationships among people that determine accountability, not policy or technology;

2. One size does not fit all;

3. Remember to focus on "what's in it for me?";

4. Different strokes for different folks; and

5. Team performance requires many people in many roles.

1. It's the Relationships Among People That Determine Accountability, Not Policy or Technology

Attention to creating and sustaining the relationships among Quality Circle members has been the key to the success of the teams. The goal—to have people contribute input to the policy development process—has become secondary to the importance of sharing information, developing communication channels with counterparts throughout the DOE community, and "getting everyone on the same page" in discussing issues of current interest. To paraphrase one workshop participant, "We're a team because we talk. Yes, we use our virtual team tools to influence policy, but more importantly, we use them to influence each other."

Team members quickly noted that access to information about one another was as important as access to information about projects, plans, and procedures. Via a shared collaborative Web portal, they created both Yellow Pages (directories of whom to call based on the sort of problem they were facing) and White Pages (directories of individual team members with digitized snapshots, biographies, current responsibilities, and significant problems they had dealt with in the past). The team began to use the "water cooler" space in their Web portal to discuss issues of common concern that transcended their Quality Circle functions. In the process, they began to evolve a community of interest.

2. One Size Does Not Fit All

In the most successful Circles, negotiating performance expectations is a process, not an event. Within general boundaries such as checking the collaborative Web space once a day, responding to e-mail according to the agreed-on priority indicators, and keeping internal Circle discussions confidential, different Circles generated unique ground rules for themselves. As an example, one Circle found it particularly important to protect their internal "devil's advocates"—people who were willing and adept at pointing out all the contrary points in a discussion. The team wanted to keep this input, but agreed that they had a history of figuratively "beating up" on any member who played this role. They asked to have an icon created of a little devil with a three-pointed spear that members could use to preface their comments when they were in a devil's advocacy role. Circle members agreed to honor that icon as representing a valid perspective in their collaborative process.

The team broke up critical expectations into three different categories. Access and response expectations specified how best to contact each team member, given time zone and technology constraints. Team members agreed on a common definition of how many hours or days were implied by labeling e-mail or voice mail "routine," "priority," or "urgent." Technology protocols clarified expectations about how individual team members would label and construct their e-mails in order to reduce info-glut in the system. General performance expectations addressed how team members would behave toward one another in consonance with the values that they had agreed on as a team. One of the most critical of these was that the team as a whole felt it was critical that internal discussions remain confidential until there was consensus on the best way to proceed. The behavioral expression of this value was that no member would "leak" to management the content of team discussions until the internal debate was finished.

3. Remember to Focus on "What's in It for Me?"

The most successful Circles have been those who were careful to pare down both their expectations and their rules to the bare minimum. The attitude they took was, "If it doesn't help us deal with our daily work, it doesn't help." Leaders in these Circles devoted significant time to understanding who members were, the work they did, the challenges they faced, the skills they had, and what kinds of information and knowledge they wanted and needed.

One common characteristic of successful DOE Circle leaders is that they have been (or are) members of the group they now lead. That gives them an in-depth understanding of what Circle members want and the issues with which they are most concerned. A second helpful characteristic has been leader willingness to invoke the stated performance expectations of the group as the means to bring wayward team members back into the fold. As one team leader put it, "We started getting better participation and more frequent contributions when I began to focus on how they could help each other rather than on what I needed from them. We use the water cooler [social comment space] to blow off steam about the time pressures. That's a release valve people find useful. It's helped us discover we have more in common than we thought."

4. Different Strokes for Different Folks

More than one Circle member has observed by collaborating using online tools that the introverts and extroverts on the team have sometimes switched roles—a fact that has significant implications when we think about leadership in the online space, since most leaders in physical communities tend to be extroverts. The consensus is that introverts sometimes are more comfortable taking the lead in asynchronous communications, depending on their confidence in both the technology and subject matter. By contrast, the extroverts in the group who used to dominate face-to-face exchanges have sometimes struggled to keep up with the collaborative flow because their strongest temptation was to "pick up the phone and call someone." Virtual Circles have learned to accommodate different communication styles by planning for a mix of synchronous, asynchronous, and face-to-face exchanges.

How did DOE do this? One of the early discussion threads on the collaborative Web portal was, "How often do we need to get together, and what is the best way to do it?" The ultimate consensus was that (travel budgets permitting) the group wanted to meet face-to-face at least once a year, hold monthly conference calls, and use online conferencing, instant messaging, and e-mail on an as-needed basis.

5. Team Performance Requires Many People in Many Roles

The number of informal roles that people are prepared to play on a virtual team is one indicator of its overall health. When people are willing to step forward to match others' interests and knowledge, to serve as experts, to prod their colleagues to contribute, and to initiate key conversations, it indicates the team is something people value and want to be part of. Some common informal roles that have evolved in the virtual Quality Circles include the following:

- *Participation Coach.* Members may take an active role in encouraging others to participate by noting, "Hey, we haven't heard from you!" or simply by using the collaborative tools more than anyone else to show how effective they can be.

- *Assumption Challenger.* As Circle members discovered they now have the power to initiate policy discussions as part of resolving day-to-day work problems, a small set of people on each team began to step forward to challenge the assumption that "the way we've always done it" is necessarily the right or most effective approach.

- *Arbitrator.* Under the old system, all policy issues were automatically "bucked up to HQ" to be resolved. As Circle members found they could now see what everyone was contributing to the policy process, they began to engage in more "sidebar discussions" of the specific concerns, situations, and constraints that prompted them to "vote" as they did. This led to some members taking on the role of arbitrator in helping different sites find a middle ground that all could live with in implementing policy.

- *Instigator.* Other members distinguish themselves by their willingness to raise important but controversial issues.

What can change leaders and consultants learn from the DOE case? Looking at the DOE Quality Circles, it's apparent that team dynamics shift their shape when mediated via technology. Three aspects in particular stand out:

Technology Is Never a Neutral Aspect of Work. The relationships that people develop, the information that they share, the identities that they form, and the balance of power are all affected by the availability, flexibility, and convenience of collaborative tools. No new tool can be introduced without impacting all these elements of the workspace. When technology is introduced without first making the business and individual case for change, without aligning the incentives with existing cultural norms, and without addressing the impact on current work processes, the typical result is that productivity drops—sometimes dramatically. At the very least, the new technology will be ignored until contradictions in "how we do things" can be addressed. Engaging the Quality Circles in designing the layout and functions of their own workspaces is one example of ways to imbed new technology in existing processes.

What Can Be Tacitly Assumed in a Face-to-Face Setting Must Be Made Explicit in the Virtual Workspace. This is in order to maintain or to improve productivity, speed, and response. People who must collaborate virtually do not easily forget or forgive lack of planning, untested assumptions, or practices that fail to take account of the needs and expectations of remote team members. It is not so much that virtual team members need an ironclad checklist in order to proceed, it's that they need ample opportunity to talk about their expectations of others, to hear and negotiate what is expected of them, and to make explicit the assumptions under which they normally operate. Through such discussions, team members can help bridge the gap of time and space by developing confidence that they are all indeed playing from the same sheet of music composed with the same end in mind. Quality Circle discussions of what roles needed to be played in order to sustain group use of the collaborative website are one example of this.

Trust Keeps the Virtual Team Together. While clearly articulated purpose and priorities help keep a team on track, trust keeps the virtual team glued together. The elements of trust not only involve honoring commitments, maintaining confidentiality, and offering honest feedback, they include developing the individual and collective discipline to adhere to the protocols the team has evolved to ensure accessibility, to receive a timely response, and to reduce information glut. A key metric for predicting virtual team success is the extent to which team members abide by the rules they have set for themselves (which are usually not a matter of organizational policy). DOE Quality Circle agreements on how to label e-mail and voice mail are a case in point.

Values, Trust, and Expectations

Gaining clarity about expectations is one of the keys to a successful virtual team. But how is this accomplished? Table 6.1 provides a tool that takes the user through a two-part process: first, important values are identified and ranked; then, specific behaviors, which will indicate whether or not a value is being upheld, are described.

Where are you prepared to invest in your values? Assume you have $100 to invest in building a shared set of team values. If you and your colleagues agree on your values, the payoff is that you will understand what you expect from one another and avoid unnecessary misunderstandings. Begin by filling out the investment sheet in Table 6.1 individually by writing in the dollar values you would assign next to the values listed. Select only your top *five* values. You may enter any amount for each value, but your total investment in your five values *must not exceed $100.*

Table 6.1. Determining Team Investment in Values

Value	$$$	Definition
Acknowledgment		Have others comment on and acknowledge contributions. Public recognition within and outside the team that what we do is important.
Balance		Readiness to honor work, family, and personal commitments.
Challenging Work		Learn about, bid on, and be part of interesting and important work, regardless of position or location.
Collective Decision Making		Willingness to discuss all-important aspects of a situation and entertain all suggestions before making a decision.
Confidentiality		Confidence in the discretion of colleagues and a willingness to keep certain conversations private.
Courtesy		Maintain a polite and professional tone in our conversations with each other regardless of the situation.
Creativity		The opportunity, encouragement, and rewards to discover or invent new ways of doing things, devise new products, and improve work practices.
Disclosure		Be forewarned if others cannot meet agreed-on expectations. Be consulted and kept in the information loop.
Equality		A level playing field in terms of access to information, opportunities to contribute, and measurement of performance.
Flexibility		Greater emphasis on the final product than on the means to get there. Allow us to work according to preferences and style as long as the work gets done.
Honesty		Team commitment to deal in facts, to be open and aboveboard about problems, and to focus on solutions rather than blame.
Honoring Commitments		Team members consistently do what they say they will do within the time limits and in the manner specified.

Table 6.1. Determining Team Investment in Values, Cont'd

Value	$$$	Definition
Humor		Ability to see the funny side in the worst situations. Take work seriously and ourselves lightly.
Inclusion		Consistent effort to work both problems and opportunities as a team, not as many different cliques. Behavior that reinforces that we are all in this together as members of one team.
Informality		Acceptance of the need to speak as individuals, not just in terms of our designated roles, without anxiety about everything that is said or written.
Model Collaboration		Leaders and team members practice the right work behaviors that they expect of others.
Ownership		Take responsibility and be accountable for the team's and one's own actions.
Play to Strengths		Awareness of what each team member does best and consciously asking each of them to contribute based on those skills.
Relevant Work		Work that has an impact, makes a difference, has meaning, and is significant to leadership and to customers.
Respect Differences		Acceptance that we don't have to be the same in order to work effectively together. Acknowledgment that different perspectives can improve the ultimate solution.
Structure		Clear and consistent boundaries and processes onto which creative thinking and individual contribution may be applied.
Support		Assistance to other team members that is given freely. Management that takes an active interest in and has constructive input to the goals of the team and its members.
Surface Problems		Courage to point out when, where, and how things are not going well without fear of retribution.
Other		
TOTAL ≤ $100		COUNT = only five values

Once each team member has completed the form, the team should meet as a group to discuss the various values selected. Team members should then come to consensus on the top five values for the team.

Values and Expectations

Next, as a team, translate the top five values you selected into statements describing specific behavior. Enter your values in rank order; the most "expensive" value should be listed as number one on a form similar to the one in Table 6.2.

Table 6.2. Prioritizing Team Values

Top Five Values	Example of Specific Behavior I Expect
1.	
2.	
3.	
4.	
5.	

However you describe the behavior that exemplifies each value, it must be evident to both you and your colleagues whether "Yes, they did it" or "No, they didn't do it." A vague statement of behavior such as, "We are always polite with one another" for the value of "courtesy" is not very helpful. It's much more useful in terms of clarifying expectations to say, "Voices are never raised in group discussions where ideas, not people, are challenged."

Summary

One of the most important lessons learned in the process of transforming face-to-face Quality Circles into virtual teams was the critical importance of making tacit assumptions about roles, rewards, and requirements explicit. Because DOE's virtual Quality Circles lacked the normal feedback mechanisms of day-to-day contact, they found it necessary to spend significantly more focused time on identifying, negotiating, and making clear their performance expectations. This two-way negotiation process brought into sharp relief many of the past communication problems that had existed between Circle representatives and DOE Headquarters personnel and helped to reinvigorate Circle member commitment to being part of the policy formation process.

About the Author

Carol Willett, *executive vice president for learning and innovation at Applied Knowledge Group, Inc., is a twenty-five year veteran of learning organizations. She focuses on translating lessons learned in technology-based collaboration into practices that ease the transition for her clients from the face-to-face environment to the virtual environment. She has authored a wide range of learning tools, simulations, assessments, workshops, and courses ranging in length from one day to a semester-long program for the University of Virginia. She has been published in the* Team and Organizational Development Sourcebooks *(McGraw-Hill, 1999, 2000, 2001) and in* Knowledge Management: Classic and Contemporary Works *(MIT, 2000). Her interactive simulation,* Lost in Cyberspace, *will be published by Jossey-Bass in 2002. Ms. Willett leads development of virtual team and collaborative products at AKG.*

7

The Whole System Transformation Conference

Fast Change for the 21st Century

Roland L. Sullivan, Linda K. Fairburn, and William J. Rothwell

"We are shifting to a knowledge-based economy. . . Expect turbulence, surprises, chance. That's what revolution brings" (Toffler, 2001).

The Challenge: A Universe Undergoing Substantial and Astonishing Change

The new business environment is revolutionary. Gone are the days of planned change, incremental change, continuous improvement, and change management. Old ways of organizing and doing business have been made irrelevant because the demands of an ever-competitive and changing environment are increasing the need for knowledge about how to lead organization change effectively (Beer & Nohria, 2000). Therefore, leaders and change agents search for meaningful and vigorous whole-system interventions from which they can take their bearings to navigate through currents that vary daily.

These times call for total system transformational processes that are fast, cheap, and deep. Kathleen Dannemiller, another organization consultant, speaks at global conferences with great eloquence, telling others that the days of trying to bring about change using problem-solving methods in small groups are over. The world is changing too quickly. Change interventions need to be integrated and need to move at the speed of change.

In essence, the new networked economy requires bold and courageous methodologies for organizations to become rewired and renewed. This chapter is about one such methodology: the Whole System Transformation Conference (WSTC).

Moreover, a WSTC event can clearly serve as a launch platform for a larger, longer-term, and more comprehensive organization change effort. A primary advantage is that many of the key people who will be heavily involved in the change receive and even help to create the message of change all at the same time (Burke, in press).

Whole System Transformation Conference

The Whole System Transformation Conference is based primarily on Kathleen Dannemiller's Whole-Scale Change ™ philosophy (Dannemiller Tyson Associates, 2000; see www.dannemillertyson.com).

So just what is a WSTC?

We have had difficulty attempting to explain and describe what the WSTC is. Those of us who began our careers as applied behavioral scientists and change artists in the 1960s had the same difficulty when we tried to describe what happened to us in T-groups. Both are profound and unique holistic learning experiences.

The T-group process released blocked individual energy. Using the same philosophical principles, we now are able to release and direct whole system energy with very large groups of people.

The following points depict the character of the WSTC. The WSTC is:

• The facilitation of several hundred, and sometimes several thousand, participants working and interacting together as a living system over a time span of two to four days;

- Distributed business and change leadership through the engagement of the entire system in relationship building, identity reframing, and change making;

- Shared information from all parts of the living system so that a new self-awareness occurs;

- Collaborative generation of whole-system intelligence;

- The right and compelling conversation that is most in the hearts and minds of all involved;

- Deep whole-system learning from the collective experience that powerfully produces high performance in individuals, teams, interteams, and the complete system;

- Integrated into the whole, ever-present disruptive energy of innovation and surprise—the new operating milieu of business;

- Exquisite action that is owned and committed to by all with a natural ease; and

- A powerful event that has no lasting impact unless it is integrated and used within a comprehensive and long-term systemic and systematic organization change and development journey.

In sum, a WSTC is an adaptable and custom-tailored wisdom-creating learning experience that often results in a paradigm shift.

Herman says, in the first chapter of this book, "The core competency of change consultants is not so much planning change, but rather, facilitating human interaction around a targeted effort, within an ever-changing universe." The WSTC attempts to do just that. The focus is on the most important here-and-now targets of the business. Action is collaboratively planned to sidestep or take advantage of the organization's present discontinuous and turbulent environment.

It does so primarily by facilitating meaningful and truth-telling conversations among individuals, between departments, through organization levels, and within the system as a whole. A *New York Times* representative said, after observing one of our conferences (led by Roland Sullivan and Kristine Quade) involving 1,400 participants, that deep and meaningful dialogue lead to committed action.

"As a system inquires into these three domains of identity, information and relationships, it becomes more self-aware. It has become connected to the truth of who it is, more connected to its environment and customers. . . . [and] the system be-comes healthier" (Wheatley, 1999, p. 77).

The WSTC is essentially a process that can be used to launch or revitalize any change effort or effectuate a business effort. WSTC is effective because it enables participants to experience the system's dynamics in a way in which they can learn how to interact with it more harmoniously.

The following are but a few of the many situations in which WSTCs have been effective:

- Strategic planning;

- Implementing turnaround and survival strategies;

- Increasing bottom-line profitability;

- Annual business planning and dissemination and development;

- Healing and vitalizing mergers and acquisitions;

- Redesigning basic work and core process;

- Bringing up or installing information technology systems;

- Creating and committing to shared values and behavior change integrated into culture development;

- Dialogue or domain-wide conversation in the management of new knowl-edge and business intelligence;

- Organizational restructuring;

- Enterprise globalization;

- Revitalizing quality programs;

- Customer service enhancement integrated into overall organizational effec-tiveness practices;

- Applied behavioral science interventions;

- Business processes improvement efforts;

- Whole-system team building;

- Strategic alliances and trans-organization development;

- New product development, including enhancing supply chain management;

- Venture capital start-up or greenfielding;

- Entire industry renewal; and
- Total country conflict resolution, visioning.

WSTC uniquely supports the above interventions because it allows fragmented parts of the organization to participate collaboratively in creating and integrating what is "to be"—while acquiring a new sense of wholeness. When we give up hanging on to our individual truth and experience, the collective wisdom of the group can emerge. It is this emergence that creates movement of energy and the possibility of whole-system transformation. People are then able to appreciate what is required of them from a system rewiring itself to perform at higher levels.

The Whole System Transformation Conference Model

In the following section, we briefly describe the seven phases in the WSTC model, shown in Figure 7.1:

1. Pre-launch;
2. Transforming the executive team;
3. Planning the conference;
4. Managing logistical support;
5. Facilitating the conference;
6. Implementing commitments and actions; and
7. Measuring the results.

1. Pre-Launch

The first step in the Pre-Launch stage is, of course, the first interview with the prospective client.

We believe that organizational leaders themselves know when the changes they are facing are important and urgent. They know it will be critical to find new ways of involving employees if changes are to be successfully integrated. Very few leaders have had a positive experience of working with a whole system, but almost all know the urgency of making major changes quickly if the organization is to survive and thrive. When you are contacted, there are questions you will want to ask

Figure 7.1. Whole-System Transformation Conference Model

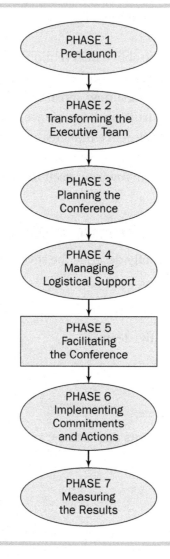

yourself and the potential client. The answers will help you to determine whether a whole-system transformation intervention is the right process to set in place, and then whether you are the right person to do the work.

Exhibit 7.1, developed in collaboration with Kathleen Dannemiller (personal correspondence, 2001), suggests a number of relevant questions when contemplating the use of WSTC.

Exhibit 7.1. Questions to Ask Yourself and the Client

When you have clarity on the following issues in your heart, soul, and head, you're on your way.

1. *Do you understand the client's problem?* This beginning question will enable you to see the world the client sees. Find out what's happening right now that is causing the client or client system to feel a profound need for change. Use questions about opportunities instead of focusing on "problems." Ask the client to describe and discuss the yearnings he or she has for changes in the organization and why he or she believes those changes will make a difference.

2. *Can you connect with the client?* Once you are able to see the world through the client's eyes, you need to ask yourself, "What drives this client? Am I able to connect with him or her? Am I ready and able to truly help achieve the changes?"

3. *Do you have the patience and commitment to truly help?* If you find that you don't agree with the client's dreams and practical needs, or if you find you don't like the client, then it is time to recommend someone else and leave. Tell the client that you don't believe you are the right person for the work that needs to be done. Recommend someone you think could be the right consultant for this particular job.

4. *What agreements do you want from the client?* If you decide you are the "right" person, then begin exploring deeper. Who will be your client? Will it be the leader, a leadership team, or possibly the human resources group? It could be any person or group that is appropriate in that particular organization. Who can help you plan and implement from inside? What are you going to need from the system if you are to be able to succeed?

5. *What must be done to ready the system?* We believe the answer to the question about readiness is contained in the invitation to come in, the agreement to go whole-system in the work, and in the contracting agreement. If you feel the need to use a whole-system approach, the client will need education such as videos, books, and opportunities to visit and talk to leaders who have used it previously. Help make sure these items are readily available.

6. *What are your wants and offers?* And last, before you actually start the work, there is some important soul-searching to do. What do you believe is the real opportunity here? Whom do you need to partner with? Do you have the time and commitment to be totally present with the work over the long haul? Are you really excited about working on this project? What are you trying to get for yourself by doing this work? Be clear about that and articulate it to yourself in order to make sure you are able to put it aside. If you don't, you could unconsciously become your own client. It's hard work to keep your own ego out of the change work.

After you have answers to these entry questions, a joint decision usually is made to go or not go with a whole-system change effort. Many transformation efforts fail because the executive leadership has not been centrally connected to the change effort. Therefore, we like to begin with leadership and then move outward to include at times major customers and stakeholders. If this "executive team" can work toward wholeness as a group, they will be a key element in the success of the WSTC.

Time Lines

While WSTCs can vary greatly from one event to the next, Table 7.1 provides a general time frame from which to visualize the entire process.

Table 7.1. WSTC Time Lines

WSTC Phase	Time Line
1. Pre-Launch	These two phases combined will take about one month
2. Transforming the Executive or Leadership Team	
3. Planning the Conference	2 to 3 days with the planning team followed within 2 to 4 weeks by another 1 to 2 days—one month total
4. Managing Logistical Support	Begins right away; the big challenge is to find a large enough space on short notice
5. Facilitating the Conference	2 to 4 days
6. Implementing Commitments and Actions	3 to 12 months following the event
7. Measuring the Results	Begins right after the executive or leadership team building and continues until one month after the event

2. Transforming the Executive or Leadership Team

We believe that a change process is likely to succeed if members of the top team can model new behaviors before they expect others to do so. Ackerman Anderson and Anderson (2001) espouse the idea that changing leaders' mindsets is critical to their ability to consciously lead the organization's transformation. It is helpful for members of the leadership team to experience their own paradigm shift so they can clearly support and successfully lead a participative change process.

Secondarily, we help them become aligned with the who, what, where, when, and how of the transformation. The crucial difference between this effort to transform a leadership team into readiness for the WSTC and traditional leadership team building is the purpose: the WSTC process involves many participants who co-create a synchronized intelligence to accomplish business results. Team building provides the executive team with new behaviors, attitudes, and the mindset to influence, and be influenced by, the whole system or organization.

After the executive team has become more cohesive, the next challenge is to do the same with the next level of leadership. We all know having leadership aligned and attuned to the transformation effort is essential. The leadership team must commit to leading the next step of the sweeping change. They must exude confidence in members at all levels of the organization to embrace and pursue the new state.

3. Planning the "Big" Conference

A conference planning team (CPT) is selected to plan the grand meeting. The team members may have their first session just before or after the executive team-building session. Ideally, they should represent as much of a cross-section of the organization as possible, and that means they should represent different functions, levels, and attitudes found in the organization. We always encourage the membership to include a few vocal critics and high-potential workers. They are to become responsible for the planning of the overall design of the conference as well as the moment-to-moment redesign that might be necessary during the conference. Exhibit 7.2 contains a list of questions you can use when beginning your work with the CPT.

One of the CPT's first tasks is to craft a "purpose and outcome" statement that serves as a foundation for creating a powerful conference experience. Because of

Exhibit 7.2. Questions to Ask the Conference Planning Team

The following are questions or foci for initial conversation as you start the work with the conference planning team (CPT).

1. What compelling change and field forces are emerging both within and outside of the system?

2. What external business climate drivers do you need to stay ahead of?

3. Where is the "hot" energy that people simply want to have a meaningful conversation about?

4. What is the missing link in all of what you are doing?

5. What internal or external turbulence are you in or about to hit?

6. What surprises have you just been faced with?

7. What possible "impacting chance or surprises" does leadership's intuition point you to—that if left unexplored may cause you to miss a huge opportunity?

8. Is there work that must be done first, that is, downsizing or change in membership of the executive or leadership team?

9. Specifically who is the client? Is it the head of the total system or of a subsystem?

10. What will be the roles of leadership, the consultant, and the conference planning team?

11. What will be the steps you can jointly agree on before and after the conference?

12. How will you evaluate success?

the diversity of the group, they are actually a rough microcosm of the organization, representing the actual current DNA of that organization. This microcosm, therefore, is able to work together to present a system-wide view to you and to each other. Their innovative abilities are tapped to plan a conference that will decidedly make a difference. The plan they develop with you, the consultant, will therefore be the best plan for this organization at this moment in time. Never have we seen two conferences designed the same. Adaptability and applied innovation are key to the success of the experience.

The CPT must reach consensus on an agenda so compelling that it will result in a true transformation for the participants in the WSTC. If one of the members is not convinced that the plan will produce a paradigm shift, rework occurs until everyone is confident that what has been created will have a far-reaching impact, an impact that will truly leave the organization shifted to the degree that it will never return to its old form.

One of us, Roland, was attempting to describe what transformation meant to a client at a major airline when his then seven-year-old daughter, Arielle, piped up in the background and said, "Dad, I know what a transformation is. It is when the caterpillar becomes the butterfly. It is changed forever and can never go back to becoming a caterpillar again." A transformed system has a new identity but still keeps that same DNA.

Kilmann, in a presentation at the 2001 Academy of Management in Washington, DC, said that transformation is a fundamental shift from one paradigm to another. A fundamental change, by definition, necessarily affects how all members of an organization see, think, and behave. Without it, a change initiative would be rather superficial and short-lived, not paradigmatic.

Through the use of positive inquiry (Watkins & Mohr, 2001) or proposing the "right" questions, consultants determine with the CPT how participants envision a newly transformed system will see, think, and behave. A carefully designed agenda is created to help move the organization from its current reality to the new state. The CPT mentally anticipates the reactions of the participants and then informs the internal and external consultants of what will and will not work in the WSTC.

You can use Exhibit 7.3 to begin the WSTC planning process.

Exhibit 7.3. Planning and Carrying Out a Whole-System Transformation Conference

Directions: *Use this worksheet to guide your thinking in planning and carrying out a Whole System Transformation Conference. For each phase of the WSTC listed in the left column below, make some notes in the right column about what you need to do to plan the conference in your organization. Be creative and complete in your response.*

Phases in Planning and Carrying Out a WSTC	What Do You Need to Do?
1. Pre-Launch	

Exhibit 7.3. Planning and Carrying Out a Whole-System Transformation Conference, Cont'd

Phases in Planning and Carrying Out a WSTC	What Do You Need to Do?
2. Transforming the Executive or Leadership Team	
3. Planning the Conference	
4. Managing Logistical Support	
5. Facilitating the Conference	
6. Implementing Commitment and Action	
7. Measuring the Results	

4. Managing Logistical Support

A well-run WSTC has sound logistical preparation and sufficient support staff. We usually like to have the logistics support team (LST) guided by an internal consultant but led by someone who is highly skilled in clerical administrative support.

The location for the conference also must be suitable, with a single meeting room of appropriate size, shape, and acoustics. Our experience has given us a space guideline to ensure that we have a large enough room. We say that you need twenty-five square feet per person. If you have a little less it will work, but if you get down to fifteen square feet, you won't be successful. If people can't hear each other at the tables, they will eventually stop participating. The facility also must be able to feed large numbers of people quickly.

Each activity on the agenda needs careful preparation, right down to the printed instructions on color-coded sheets. Prior to the event, a logistics team leader choreographs each step of the agenda with the needed materials and the movements of a floor support team. Members of the LST are kept quite busy. For example, they deliver materials to tables and then type and copy data generated in the activities for subsequent table work. For large conferences, three shifts cover the full twenty-four hours. The membership of the LST can be drawn either internally from any part of the organization or externally from contractors or interested stakeholders.

5. Facilitating a Conference

On the first day of the event, a big meeting room is filled with round tables to accommodate hundreds or thousands of people meeting in table groups of six to ten. Sometimes, coordinated conferences are happening concurrently at some other location in the world. In that case, the big rooms are connected via satellite TV.

Activities link the work of individuals to their table groups, and special processes and methods link the small groups to the whole system. The key is to get participants talking and working with each other as part of the whole system.

One of the keys to success is working in table teams. Membership at the table is carefully selected to form a team that is as diverse as possible. The more varied the views from the whole system, the better.

Because so much preparation is done in advance, as few as two professional facilitators, one external and one internal, can effectively manage very large groups. We also believe that the competence of the facilitators is critical. In the last few years, fewer organizations are doing large interactive conferences. We believe this is due to lack of highly skilled large-group facilitators.

One of the best preparations for facilitating large groups is substantial experience in facilitating small groups. What we do in the WSTC is based essentially on what the change field has learned from small-group dynamics since the 1960s (Bradford, Gibb, & Benne, 1964). Unlike small-group facilitation, which can be flexible in the moment, large-group design must be thorough and require very little or no redesign on the spot. Redesign can happen at breaks or overnight.

In spite of the large numbers of participants, the WSTC is every bit as interactive as a team-building or small-group planning session. Everyone needs to be fully engaged in the process to ensure its success.

If the CPT has written an excellent agenda—we call it a script—along with clear instructions for table work, the participants begin to facilitate themselves. If the instructions are not clear, the entire room could go into confusion. Therefore, when we realize that a few tables are confused, we get on the microphone and go over the instructions again. This small intervention can save the day.

Table groups share information, either person-to-person or by one of the technologies mentioned below, and the room becomes a human database that is churned into applied behavioral science wisdom. New behavior and thought structures are experienced and agreed on. Core organization processes and structure are often transfigured. Participants buy into action plans that they help to develop.

Depending on the size of the system, the conference may be used once or many times to fit the needs of the organization. Individual conferences can be serial or sequential. In serial events, members divide into segments and all experience the same agenda at different points in time—say the first segment meets one week and another segment the next week. In sequential events, planners define a broad set of tasks and all participants begin in one event and continue in the next. The first conference might work on setting and finalizing the strategy, while subsequent conferences might each work on the implementation of a specific strategy or redesign of a core process.

In large organizations, it may not be possible to include all the organization's members in a single event, so planners develop several events scheduled close enough together to keep the organization moving forward together and creating a critical mass for change. A power company in the western United States held four WSTCs with five hundred participants in each during a one-month period. Another non-U.S. organization planned two large events for the top of the organization and then eight in its business units.

New technology can facilitate WSTCs in some of the following ways:

- We now have each person or each table team interlinked through their computers to very powerful software that can be used to mine the data from everyone involved. The software reads common phrases and instantly reflects back core issues and commonalities to the actual database.

- Facilitators can generate questions on the spot for the entire conference to answer. Varying degrees of sophisticated analysis can occur right in front of the participants. Creative graphics and charts can result from the analysis; participants can then go into deeper and deeper cycles of conversation and action generation.

- Satellite TV connects the room with other locations from around the world. Recently we were involved in a conference where dozens of remote sites from around the world came in live to the central room.

- Wireless laptop computers and other hand-held devices at each table can replace easel pads, allowing for more descriptive and comprehensive report-outs on conference-hall-sized screens.

- Individuals can send each other private instant messages in the room or instant message to another part of the world to acquire needed information. We just had a situation where a subordinate sent her boss a real-time message. The boss heard a faint chime on her wireless handheld, clicked it, and there was her subordinate at the back of the room telling her live on video to stop dominating the panel presentation.

- Documentation of essential takeaways is also more complete. In some cases, plans can go right into enterprise project management databases to be tracked and measured. In one case where a task was overdue, the boss and the person responsible automatically received an e-mail reminder!

- Entire rooms can be connected to the Web or to the company intranet to utilize virtual meeting technology or to explore company reports or see real-time production. The leader in the center of the room can take charge of all computers and actually control the mouse on each and every computer.

- Instant group messaging can occur with remote sites around the world.

- Consultants can switch conversations instantaneously from those involving the entire conference to subgroups or divisions.

- Live video can project individual or small-group presentations to the entire room from any spot in the room or in the world.

- Group decision support systems have moved from simple "yes or no" responses to the generation of conference wisdom through software that "thinks" by making and synthesizing statistical correlations. Survey feedback designs can be created and administered and results can be made available within the twinkle of an eye.

Watch for an explosion of technology over the next five years. Different applications are starting to be combined in such a way that the conference itself becomes a genie in a bottle. The new organic chips now in development will create a holistic and expanded memory base that will provide capabilities presently beyond our imaginations. A real competitive edge will belong to those companies that first utilize the incredible data management that is just beginning to emerge.

A wonderful technology resource for large meetings and organization change consulting can be found at www.execusurv.com.

Warning! Technology, if not used appropriately, can get in the way of heartfelt conversation and kill the energy that is emerging. One of the reasons large interactive meetings work is because people have a new sense of connecting personally to the whole. When individuals speak with passion stemming from their innermost beings, they psychologically connect and bond with others.

6. Implementing Commitments and Actions

It's common for teams intimately connected with a WSTC—the executive and conference planning teams—to become members of the implementation team. They often have considerable assistance from enthusiastic participants and so find themselves delegating tasks as well as working on particular substantive issues. The following substantive tasks are common in the implementation phase:

- *Diffusion and Deployment of Decisions.* Some organizations must telegraph changes, such as new work processes, to affiliates or to remote parts of the organization.

- *Pursue Action Plans.* Most WSTCs end with the creation of action plans. These are the first steps to real process change. Immediately following the conference, cross-functional work groups that have been appointed by management or that have become self-organized are primed to work on and refine those action plans. Such implementation teams ensure coordination and accountability of follow-up activities.

- *Reinforce Practice.* It is one thing to articulate new cultural values and practice them in an offsite environment. It is quite another to establish firm habits of behavior that will maintain the paradigm shift and grow that culture. Leaders must reinforce and model the new behavior.

- *Temporarily Institutionalize Structures for Change.* An organization will not come out of a WSTC the same as it went in. A feeling of accomplishment has occurred, and tremendous energy has been released. The organization may need to modify or create new processes while major processes will require integration. Leaders must grasp this opportunity to build their organization's capacity into daily operations, such as annual business planning.

7. Measuring Results

At a WSTC conducted by Roland Sullivan and Kristine Quade, the client spent hundreds of thousands of dollars using outside research firms to conduct pre- and post-test measurements around culture change and customer satisfaction. The findings were that significant positive improvement occurred. The largest financial institution in South Africa conducted a pilot WSTC in one of its fifty divisions before it was used at the top. The pilot division increased profits 69 percent in four and one-half months, which resulted in an additional $30M in profit to the bottom line.

In a successful conference, change occurs in how participants interact. Change that is barely perceptible at first may become resoundingly clear as the conference draws to a close. People start to believe in each other and gain ways of understanding and working together. Participants take down barriers and put in place a rich web that weaves the organization together in a profound and fundamental way. Confidence emerges that participants themselves can resolve their own problems. Successful conferences effect a paradigm shift of the first magnitude. These special skills and learnings—from new ways of interacting with co-workers to conducting better meetings—become part of the organization's new culture.

Dr. Michael Arena (2000), the continuous improvement director for Glen-Gery Corporation, recently presented research findings from three case studies that employed Whole-Scale Change™/WSTC technology. He concluded the following:

- The cycle time of change accelerated and the level of commitment to change increased through the process of engaging employees;

- The methodology of large-group change provides the forum to initiate and mobilize an organization toward establishing system-wide solutions versus the traditional piecemeal approach;

- Organizational barriers were reduced so that system members could participate fully, which precipitated an increase in the level of enthusiasm;

- The creation of space that occurred during these large conferences provided the opportunity for connections to occur;

- More meaningful relationships, better information, and a shared identity resulted;

- Enhanced relationships helped to unify the organization, while the information was used to improve the whole system, and the newly shared identity acted as a unifying force long after the events;

- This methodology generated significant emotional charge and increased the level of organizational awareness. The awareness enhanced the understanding of the organization's strategy, individual group needs, the case for change, and each individual's role within the larger system; and

- The process generated a sense of hope that evolved from a high degree of ownership, enthusiasm, and energy.

WSTC Team Requirements

Four types of teams are referred to throughout this chapter and are required for the successful implementation of a WSTC. These are the *executive or leadership team, conference planning team, logistics support team,* and the *implementation team.* See Table 7.2 for a description of each team's composition.

Table 7.2. WSTC Teams and Their Composition

Team Type	Composition
Executive or Leadership Team	5 to 12 chief officers or the lead management team and the internal consultant(s)
Conference Planning Team	10 to 25 people comprising 1 or 2 members of the executive or leadership team and a cross-section of the organization representing various functions, levels, attitudes, and geographies

Table 7.2. WSTC Teams and Their Composition, Cont'd

Team Type	Composition
Logistics Support Team	Internal consultants, administrative support staff, technical specialists, external volunteers, and interested parties from other parts of the organization
Implementation Team	Representatives from the executive or leadership team and conference planning teams, possibly those selected by management or conference participants and those passionately self-selected

Conceptual Framework and Underpinning Philosophy

A multitude of whole system transformation theories have formed the basis for our work. An essential recipe that has driven us is Gleicher's formula (see Beckhard & Prichard, 1992), shown below:

$$SCE = D \times V \times Sfs \times B$$

In this formula:

- SCE is the chance for Success of a Change Effort;

- D is the degree of Dissatisfaction of all significant parties with the current state;

- V is the Vision of the desired state;

- Sfs is the Strategy for taking the First Steps; and

- B is the degree to which key members Believe that the change effort will produce desired results.

(For a more complete explanation of the above formula, see pages 167–174 in *Finding Your Way in the Consulting Jungle: A Guide for OD Practitioners,* by Freedman and Zackrison.)

In 1966, Barbara Bunker and Billie Alban (1997) identified a dozen or so major large-group interventions. Since then, many of those methods for engaging the whole system for rapid change have assimilated each other's values, techniques, theory, and models. Innovation has occurred as large-group interactive events have evolved into a whole-system change and development process. The best resource for many of the other contemporary group-change methods is *The Change Handbook,* by Holman and Devane (1999). This book presents chapters about each of the whole-system technologies currently in use.

Peter Block (2000)–long noted for being the trainer of change consultants— distills the current state of the whole-system approach:

- There are times when the people affected by the change can join you in the discovery, recommendation, decision, and implementation. This is the whole-system approach.

- The essence of whole-system discovery is to get everyone in the room at the same time.

- The main advantage is that there is no need to sell a set of actions to anyone. . . . People will resist change being inflicted on them.

- The power of the whole-system approach lies not so much in management sponsorship but in the high engagement and involvement of the entire organization.

- The value of the whole-system approach is that it engages entire units to self-assess their current reality and plan how to improve it. Making a choice about a consulting strategy, then, means deciding whether to give priority to the special expertise and neutrality of the consultant, which leads to a third-party approach, or give priority to people's commitment to implementation, which might tilt the scales toward a whole-systems approach. (pp. 210–211)

We believe that best practice must be based on sound theory. The WSTC is based primarily on the theory and concepts of the following people's research: Kathleen Dannemiller, Richard Beckhard, Jack Gibb, Ron Lippitt, John and Joyce Weir, Margaret Wheatley, and Warner Burke. See www.rolandsullivan.com for an expanded exposition. Over the years, we have sprinkled in a dozen or so of the other whole-system approaches. Our favorites include the following:

- Future Search (see www.futuresearch.net)

- Appreciative Inquiry (see www.appreciativeinquiry.cwru.edu)

- Margaret Wheatley's Approach (see www.margaretwheatley.com)

Conclusion

We believe we will experience more change in the next thirty years than since the beginning of civilization. With nano-technology and a wireless world just around the corner, the pace of change will quicken to unimaginable rates. Top-down cascading methods of organization change take too long and are too costly. Change is disquieting when done *to* a system, but enlivening and enlightening when consciously done *by* the entire system. Creating change just for executive teams or small change teams is no longer efficient or effective. Cummings and Worley (2001) have identified large-group interventions as the fastest growing type of consulting interventions. One of those is the WSTC. The large-scale, simultaneous participation of many people from the organization in a change effort reduces resistance and results in exhilaration, motivation, ownership, and the ability to implement with commitment.

We believe that the WSTC is an approach that responds both to Toffler's (2001) prediction of surprise, turbulence, and chance for the upcoming years and Drucker's visionary view of change: "Every organization will have to become a change leader. You can't manage change. You can only be ahead of it" (Drucker & Senge, 2001).

For years, change agents have helped people to experience paradigm shifts in T-groups and in small groups in residential team building. That was then. Now we are just beginning to explore the possibilities of how paradigm shifting can be experienced by large numbers of people through whole-system approaches.

One of our favorite clients, Chuck Blitzer, CEO of MGI Pharma, uses a race car analogy as he describes how the company sees itself moving forward into the future: "We have our pedal fully to the metal and occasionally lightly touch the brake. The WSTC provides the track and the crash walls so we might quicken our steps into a wildly exciting and bodacious future" (personal correspondence, 2001). We believe the WSTC allows organizations to stay ahead of the proliferation of changes, driving in fast-forward with all stakeholders freely engaged while reducing the risk of a crash.

References

Ackerman Anderson, L., & Anderson, D. (2001). *The change leader's roadmap: How to navigate your organization's transformation.* San Francisco: Jossey-Bass/ Pfeiffer.

Arena, M.J. (2000). *A study of whole-scale change: Trading in the tradeoff.* Cincinnati: The Union Institute.

Beckhard, R., & Harris, R. (1987). *Organizational transitions: Managing complex change.* Reading, MA: Addison-Wesley.

Beckhard, R., & Prichard, W. (1992). *Changing the essence: The art of creating and leading fundamental change in organizations.* San Francisco: Jossey-Bass.

Beer, M., & Nohria, N. (2000). *Breaking the code of change.* Boston: Harvard Business School Press.

Block. P. (2000). *Flawless consulting: A guide to getting your expertise used* (2nd ed.). San Francisco: Jossey-Bass/Pfeiffer.

Bradford, L., Gibb, J., & Benne, K. (1964). *T-group theory and laboratory method.* New York: John Wiley & Sons.

Bunker, B.B., & Alban, B.T. (1997). *Large group interventions: Engaging the whole system for rapid transformation.* San Francisco: Jossey-Bass.

Burke, W.W. (in press). *Organization change: Theory and practice.* Thousand Oaks, CA: Sage.

Cummings, T., & Worley, C. (2001). *Organization development & change* (7th ed.). Cincinnati: South-Western.

Dannemiller Tyson Associates (2000*). Whole-scale change: Unleashing magic in organizations.* San Francisco: Berrett-Koehler.

Drucker, P., & Senge, P. (2001). *A conversation with Peter Drucker & Peter Senge: Leading in a time of change* (video). New York: The Drucker Foundation/San Francisco: Jossey-Bass.

Freedman, A., & Zackrison, R. (2001). *Finding your way in the consulting jungle: A guidebook for organization development practitioners.* San Francisco: Jossey-Bass/Pfeiffer.

Gibb, J.R. (1972). The TORI community experience as an organizational change intervention. In W.W. Burke (Ed*.), Contemporary organization development.* Washington, DC: NTL Institute for Applied Behavioral Science.

Holman, P., & Devane, T. (1999). *The change handbook: Group methods for shaping the future.* San Francisco: Berrett-Koehler.

Kilmann, R. (2001). *Quantum organizations: A new paradigm for achieving organizational success and personal meaning.* Palo Alto, CA: Davies-Black.

Quade, K., Giacobassi, J., Miner, L., Sullivan, R., Symons, J., Turner, T., Weiser, K., Wind, L., & Wrede, E. (1996*). The essential handbook: Behind the scenes of large group interactive events.* Deephaven, MN: Sullivan Publishing Group.

Rothwell, W.J., Prescott, R., & Taylor, M. (1998). *The strategic HR leader.* Palo Alto, CA: Davies-Black.

Rothwell, W.J., Sanders, E.S., & Soper, J.G. (1999). *ASTD models for workplace learning and performance: Roles, competencies and outputs.* Alexandria, VA: American Society for Training and Development.

Rothwell, W.J., Sullivan, R., & McLean, G.N. (Eds.). (1995). *Practicing organization development: A guide for consultants.* San Francisco: Jossey-Bass/Pfeiffer.

Senge P., Roberts, C., Ross, R., Smith, B., Roth, G., & Kleiner, A. (1999). *Dance of change: The challenges to sustaining momentum in a learning organization.* New York: Doubleday.

Srivastva, S. & Cooperrider, D.L. (1999). *Appreciative management and leadership: The power of positive thought in organizations.* Euclid, OH: Williams Custom Publishing.

Toffler, A. (2001, August 27). America's future: The mood now. *Newsweek*, p. 76.

Watkins, J., & Mohr, B. (2001). *Appreciative inquiry: Change at the speed of imagination.* San Francisco: Jossey-Bass/Pfeiffer.

Wheatley, M. (1999). *Leadership and the new science: Discovering order in a chaotic world* (2nd ed.). San Francisco: Berrett-Koehler.

About the Authors

Roland L. Sullivan, *MSOD, has worked for thirty-five years externally as an organization change consultant. His degrees are in philosophy and organization change. His professional competence is essentially geared toward whole-system change, learning, and renewal. Blending hard-hitting business results and development of human and technical systems underpin his work. Those who know Mr. Sullivan experience his passion for large-group dynamics.*

In the mid-1970s, he founded the Minnesota Organization Development Network. He has been honored by his colleagues as the Minnesota OD Practitioner of the Year, as a Wisdom Keeper by the Minnesota ASTD chapter, and he was named International OD Consultant of the Year at the 17th World OD Congress by the OD Institute.

For the past twenty years, he has based his work on a consistent message: More change will occur in the remainder of our lifetimes than has taken place since the beginning of civilization.

On a personal note, Mr. Sullivan would like to acknowledge the tremendous influence that Stan Herman and his work on authentic management has had on him.

Mr. Sullivan can be contacted at the following address: 20020 Vine Street, Deephaven, MN 55331, phone: 952–474–8363, e-mail: Roland@rolandsullivan.com.

Linda K. Fairburn, *MSOD, is a consultant, trainer, and educator in the areas of organization development, adult education, and individual, team, and business transformation. She draws on her practical experience as founder and president of companies in the service and manufacturing sectors, integrating hands-on skills in management with a client's perspective of change issues.*

Supporting her entrepreneurial capabilities are a bachelor's degree in education and art therapy from the University of Waterloo, Ontario, and in adult education from St. Francis Xavier University, Nova Scotia, and a master of science in organization development (MSOD) from Pepperdine University in California.

Ms. Fairburn develops and writes workshops of all descriptions for numerous organizations and is the co-author of the book, Exit Right: A Guided Tour of Succession Planning for Families-in-Business-Together *(with M. Voeller & W. Thompson) (Summit Run, 2002). As a citizen of both Canada and the United States, she travels and works freely with clients on both sides of the border, as well as in Southwest Asia, in the areas of organization development, change, and family business succession planning.*

Ms. Fairburn can be contacted at the following address: 170 University Avenue West, Suite 12-129, Waterloo, Ontario, Canada N2L 3E9, phone: 519–749–2218, www.makingthingshappen.net, e-mail: lido@kw.igs.net.

William J. Rothwell, Ph.D., *is professor of human resources development in the department of adult education, instructional systems and workforce education and development in the College of Education on the University Park Campus of the Pennsylvania State University. Before arriving at Penn State in 1993, he was assistant vice president and management development director for a major insurance company, and before that training director in a state government agency. He has worked full-time in human resources management and employee training and development from 1979 to the present.*

Dr. Rothwell received his Ph.D. with a specialization in human resources development from the University of Illinois at Urbana-Champaign, his MBA with a specialization in human resources management from Sangamon State University (now called the University of Illinois at Springfield), his M.A. from the University of Illinois at Urbana-Champaign, and his B.A. from Illinois State University. He holds lifetime accreditation as a Senior Professional in Human Resources (SPHR) and was once accredited as a Registered Organization Development Consultant (RODC). His latest publications include The Manager and Change Leader *(2001, ASTD Press);* Effective Succession Planning, *2nd ed. (2000, AMACOM);* The Competency Toolkit *(with David Dubois) (2000, HRD Press);* Building In-House Leadership and Management Development Programs: Their Creation, Management, and Continuous Improvement *(with H.C. Kazanas) (1999, Quorum Press);* ASTD Models for Workplace Learning and Performance *(with E. Sanders & J. Soper) (1999, ASTD Press);* The Action Learning Guidebook *(1999, Jossey-Bass/Pfeiffer); and* The Sourcebook for Self-Directed Learning *(edited with K. Sensenig) (1999, HRD Press).*

Dr. Rothwell can be contacted at the following address: Pennsylvania State University, 305C Keller Building, University Park, PA 16802–3202, phone: 814–863–2581, e-mail: wjr9@psu.edu.

Part 4

HR, OD, and Information Technology

ON PART 4, WE LOOK AT TWO OTHER EFFECTS of the emergence imperative: (1) the development of new Internet-based tools and (2) the burgeoning of new job configurations.

In Chapter 8, Perry Nelson presents a broad array of basic information technology resources for managers, consultants, and others responsible for guiding organization transition efforts. In Chapter 9, Jana Markowitz points out the ways in which job roles and responsibilities are radically altered as technology and business needs give birth to new mixtures of job responsibilities that combine to require both technical and human organizational skills. The mutual impacts of information technology and human resources functions are particularly examined.

8

Basic Info-Tech for Consultants

Perry Nelson

AS ORGANIZATIONS REWIRE THEMSELVES for the networked economy, consultants who serve those organizations also face the challenge of learning to use the tools of information technology if they hope to keep pace in the economy of the 21st Century. Large consulting organizations often help their consulting staff achieve this goal by providing them the electronic tools, both hardware and software, they need to link to their clients. Perhaps more importantly, they provide the technical support needed to research the appropriate tools, to train people in how to use them effectively, and to troubleshoot them when there are problems. And yet even this level of commitment to information technology poses a considerable challenge to employees in those organizations. Skill in a particular consulting specialty does not necessarily translate into a facility for learning about and using technological tools or into an open-minded willingness to accept a new way of doing things.

However, the kind of technical support and access to the latest tools that employees of large consulting organizations have puts them at a distinct advantage over their counterparts in smaller ones. The employees in small consulting firms face an even more daunting challenge in keeping pace with their clients' transition to the networked economy. Without technical specialists to investigate and recommend which tools might be most useful or to teach them the ins and outs of how to use them, consultants in these smaller organizations are left to their own ingenuity. They must find, implement, and learn the tools on their own as they continue to serve their clients' needs without missing a beat. It is to this harried group of consultants that we primarily direct this chapter.

It is important to keep in mind that the best way to use the capability offered by information technology in the consulting process is yet to be determined. Some consultants have begun to explore ways to consult electronically with clients in networked organizations, but newly emerging tools still offer an opportunity for you to pioneer which consulting activities may be enhanced most by these capabilities. However far behind you may feel you are at the moment, if you begin now, you can still be on the leading edge of the curve. The promise of the technology is that mastering these new tools may provide new opportunities for remote collaboration and availability, and, as you integrate these tools into your daily work, your clients will recognize that your electronic availability adds value to your service.

In this chapter we'll introduce some ways to use the basic tools of information technology to your advantage in your consulting practice, and we'll provide some tips about how to become current and to keep up with the explosive growth of technology. We'll open a door to the world of consulting in the networked economy.

Master the Use of E-Mail

The most common information technology tool of the online world, e-mail, can be one of the most powerful if it is used properly. Because of the asynchronous nature of e-mail communication (that is, the recipient can read it and respond to it at a time when it is convenient to do so), it provides an easy way to stay in touch with one's contacts and with other decision makers within a client organization. Among the advantages that it offers are that it is cheap, almost effortless, and nearly instantaneous. (Ironically, those advantages can also lead to some of the potential pitfalls of using it, but more about those later.)

Most people who are online have become accustomed to sending and receiving e-mail, so it has a familiarity that makes it less intimidating than other info-tech tools. Listing your e-mail address on your business card is now commonplace, and one doesn't even have to own a computer to have an e-mail address. Services like Microsoft's Hotmail, Yahoo, Excite, or Mail.com all offer free e-mail addresses that can be accessed from any computer anywhere in the world. Since e-mail has become so ubiquitous, consultants often make use of it to negotiate working agreements with associates, conduct surveys or interviews with groups or individuals, or plan strategies for deploying various implementations within an organization. They also frequently use it to get feedback on ideas or sometimes, within organizations, to conduct 360-degree feedback with members of their groups.

E-mail is faster than hard copy forms of communication, and it offers some advantages that no other means of communication does. For instance, one can attach a document to an e-mail that can be easily manipulated after it is received. Voice messages, photographs, presentations, word processing or spreadsheet documents, or video files can enhance the communication simply by being sent as attachments to an e-mail. This ability to send attachments makes collaboration on projects more feasible than ever before for people who are widely dispersed. In writing this book for example, the authors, though located in various places around the world, were able to attach drafts of our chapters to the e-mail messages we exchanged so as to permit others to react to and comment on the development of the work. Although the advent of the fax machine provided a vehicle for almost instantaneous communication, the faxed document isn't in a format that can be manipulated, edited, and built upon once it arrives at its destination.

Yet for all of its advantages and its familiarity, e-mail is easy to abuse in the business context.

A recent *New York Times* article indicated that "E-mail remains the most popular online application, with more than 6.1 billion messages sent daily" (Headlam, 2001). Given this flood of daily e-mail, it is easy to be overcome by it even at one's personal e-mail address. When you think about the volume of e-mail one receives at work, it is not hard to understand why people develop a dread of looking in their own in-boxes. The wise consultant will therefore learn to use e-mail judiciously.

Although it may be tempting to try to develop rapport with a client by forwarding jokes or other nonbusiness related amusements, avoid that trap. You risk overwhelming your client with messages that aren't of high priority but that still require valuable work time to process. Or worse, you might even alienate the client if your sense of what's funny isn't exactly on target. Try to use e-mail in such a way as to cause your client to look forward to the messages you send because they provide substantive and useful information. If this advice seems like an "all work and no play" philosophy, just bear in mind that time is the most precious resource one has. In the end, your client will appreciate your respecting that fact.

Remember the persistence of the digital record. E-mail gets backed up from a company's servers frequently, usually daily. It can be forwarded to others. It can be subpoenaed and read in court when disputes arise. So don't treat it casually. E-mail is easy to dash off, as if it were merely chatting, or to send without checking for spelling errors or poor grammar. However, it may well last longer and be distributed more widely than any other official written communications you have with a client. With business e-mail it is especially important to write thoughtfully and carefully. Writing a message, letting it sit overnight, and then rereading it before you send it out the next day can save you embarrassment and sometimes even the loss of a client. And never write a business e-mail when you aren't in control of all your faculties, such as when you are home on the weekend after having relaxed with a few drinks. Once an e-mail is sent, you can't get it back. You should treat business e-mail with the same respect and gravity that you would treat your response to a request for a proposal.

The final caution is that e-mail and the attachments sent with it could spread computer viruses and worms. One sure way to alienate your client is to permit a virus to slip through your defenses and infect the client's computers. You need to exercise assiduous computer hygiene to make sure you do your best to never threaten your client company's computer security. A good virus-scanning program with up-to-date virus definition files is an absolute must.

Use the Internet
Learn to Search the Internet Effectively

The Internet is virtually an unlimited source of information about almost any subject. One valuable way you can serve your client is to share the results of your online discoveries about topics of mutual interest. But before you can share information, you must first find it. And although you will come across some useful information just by keeping your eyes open when you are surfing, you'll be a much greater asset if you have the skill to search for information purposefully. Internet search engines make that possible.

Fortunately, simple searches on the Internet are quite easy, and, with a little practice, even complex ones can get quite specific results. Teaching you how to conduct searches on the Internet is beyond the scope of this chapter, but a number of websites have already undertaken that task. The website, http:// nuevaschool.org/~debbie/library/research/adviceengine.html, for instance, provides a series of links to various search engines and comments on which of them are most appropriate to different kinds of searches. If you click on the link to the tutorial on that page, you'll receive an animated eighty-three-slide presentation of ways to use this particular page to search effectively. Danny Sullivan, who is the editor and webmaster of Search Engine Watch, provides several links to Web searching tips at http://searchenginewatch.com/facts/index.html. The time you invest in learning how to perform searches will pay off quickly and handsomely when you need to find some specific information for a project you may be doing with a client.

For example, I was once involved in a project with a client in the utility industry who wanted to help his customer-contact employees understand and be able to discuss utility deregulation with the company's customers. So he asked that I help him create a program that he chose to call "The Customer Has a Choice." While doing the research on this project, I used the Google search engine (www.google.com) and typed in "utility deregulation" for my search term. Google returned 15,300 "hits." When I added another element (Indiana) to the original search term to narrow the search somewhat (the search terms were now "utility deregulation" + "Indiana"), I got 822 hits in 0.22 seconds. This much more manageable and relevant list provided a way to focus in on information that my client and I could use in the project. Of course, one still must pick and choose among the search results those sites that match the need and visit them to read what they have to offer. But this kind of searching is much quicker and frequently more productive than poring over a card catalog in the local public library.

A number of Web portals (websites designed to be selected by users as their homepage) like www.yahoo.com, www.excite.com, or www.msn.com provide pages of links to other sites on the Web. Similarly, websites like www.ceoexpress.com and the New York Times Navigation page (requires registration), www.nytimes.com/library/tech/reference/cynavi.html, can be quick ways to navigate the Web.

No matter how you search for information on the Internet, however, you'll want to e-mail that information to your clients as links to articles, websites, or databases that you've found in your research. Or, as you become more adept at using the Web, you can post such links on your own website.

Investigate What the Internet Enables You to Do

It stands to reason that the more you know about the Internet the more you'll be able to use it to facilitate your work with your clients. While it is unlikely you will ever master the vastness of this continually expanding universe of links, becoming familiar with some of the major services it offers can inspire you to use those services creatively in your consulting work. Therefore, think of the online world as a subject worthy of study in and of itself.

If your consulting experience, like mine, has been filled with projects in which you were challenged to devise a way to achieve the objective of the engagement from the ground up, you'll find that using the Internet to supplement your other consulting activities will have a familiar feeling. However, it should be obvious that your client isn't likely to lead you into these electronic interactions and interventions. You'll have to propose, encourage, and guide them into the process.

As we've already said, the use of the Internet to facilitate consulting activities is still in its infancy, so there are no rules as yet chiseled in stone about how to put it to use. The good news about that is that, while there are no clear guidelines about what to do or how to use these tools, there are also no taboos either. You will get to discover ways to use these tools that no one else has yet tried.

Even as you search for ways to use these new tools, you'll need to make sure you don't fall into the trap of abandoning your other tools once you've discovered the electronic ones. E-mail doesn't (and shouldn't) replace telephone conversations; electronic interactions will never replace your visits to the client's premises; and the relationship with your client will still require some socialization away from work over dinner, drinks, or some other away-from-the-office activities. If your client feels you have abandoned these traditional points of contact, the electronic bridge you seek to build will become instead an electronic barrier between you.

Learn About and Experience Participating in Online Conferences

Online conferences will surely come into wider use in the future. Online conference facilitation organizations such as Caucus Systems (www.caucus.com) or Placeware (www.placeware.com) provide hosting services that make it possible for a group to conduct a conference with participants from all over the world without anyone ever having to leave home. People log on at their convenience during a specified time frame and participate in all the activities that are taking place. And everyone doesn't have to be logged on at the same time. Because of the asynchronous nature of these conferences, individuals can carry on dialogue, view presentations, or otherwise participate in the activities whenever their schedules permit.

Even when you take into consideration that you lose the value of face-to-face contact and social interactions by participating in electronic conferences, it is hard to deny the compensatory benefits these online conferences provide. For instance, they save the travel costs normally associated with attending conferences in brick-and-mortar locations, and that means more people can participate in them than if an organization had to pay for transportation and lodging. To compensate for the absence of traditional face-to-face interaction, all conference attendees can post biographical information or pictures of themselves so that everyone can get to know others better in some ways than in traditional conferences. Conference participants can provide links to other information on the Web in their comments, thus providing an enhancement that is generally unavailable at live events in the nonvirtual world. Presenters at these online conferences can post slide shows or white papers on the Web to accompany their presentations and make that material and other notes available for download so that the burden of distributing handouts is eliminated. Finally, and perhaps most significantly, a compact disc of the proceedings can provide each participant a permanent summary that documents everything that went on at a conference.

Although participating in online conferences can be intimidating to the uninitiated, the creators of these sites take care to make sure that the people can find their way around without feeling lost. Typically a help link is available on each page that explains how to use the various facilities that the conference offers. A well-designed conference site makes participation, either to post a comment or to view a presentation, just a matter of clicking on a link and typing.

It is a good idea for those who are new to such online activities to spend some time just observing, or lurking as it is called. This initial period of observation can help you become comfortable with the topics and the style of the conference. As a matter of online etiquette, experienced users are quick to offer help to those who are just learning. In the end, however, the best way to overcome inexperience is to dive in, once you are comfortable doing so, and experiment. You can't break anything, and a spirit of adventure and experimentation will serve you well in these activities.

If possible, arrange with your employer to participate in these events during your workday, rather than on your own time. The experience will be much more rewarding than if you must try to do this as an additional task. The time you invest in investigating this kind of resource will pay handsome dividends to you and your company over time.

Establish a Presence for Yourself on the Web

Even if you do not think of yourself as a "techie," your consulting practice will benefit greatly if you have a website to which you can post things you want to share with your clients or associates. Many people resist taking this step because they believe they must create a flashy site with a lot of bells and whistles. And, of course, that belief leads them to delay or avoid doing it because they don't think they have the skills necessary for such a tour de force. In my view, that is a mistaken approach, first because it is a nonstarter obstacle and secondly because it isn't necessary to build that kind of website. It is almost an axiom about the World Wide Web that content is king, but new webmasters are almost always seduced by the desire to produce a website that wows visitors with dazzling graphics. Those kinds of things can always be added later, because they are truly only decoration. If you produce a website and keep it current by mastering the skill of posting information to it when you have something new to share, that site will quickly prove valuable to those who visit it. And producing such a website is much easier than you may think.

Several companies like Geocities (www.geocities.com) and Tripod (www.tripod.com) host websites for free. These free services provide an excellent way to learn to put up Web pages. In the case of Tripod, they provide up to fifty megabytes of webspace, which is plenty large enough to house a website containing many different pages and elements. The hosting services frequently provide their own website creation tools that make the process of creating a site feasible for even the most novice webmaster. Although you might prefer to have your own domain name, such as www.TheBestConsultantEver.com, that, too, can come later. As a starting point, you will do well to set up a website at one of these free hosting services just to establish a place on which you can post things and with which you can learn the skills you need as a webmaster. A really excellent free tool to use in creating your website is the free program made available by Trellix Corporation (www.trellix.com). Although even this tool has a learning curve, it gracefully handles all of the tasks necessary for posting to the Web hosting service. Once you've set it up, adding pages to your website is no more complicated than using a word processor.

There are other alternatives for creating a website, of course. Almost every Internet service provider (ISP) includes in its costs webspace for you to put up a website. The amount of webspace available is typically limited to something like five or six megabytes. Even this limited amount of space is sufficient to learn how to post to the Web. A number of Web authoring tools, such as Microsoft's FrontPage, Macromedia's Dreamweaver, or NetObject's Fusion, provide the software tools needed to create websites without having to code the pages directly. Any of these programs give you extensive capability to create even very feature-rich websites.

Although it may not be immediately apparent what kind of information you might want to post on the Web, once you have the place and the skill to do so, the potential content will become much more obvious. For instance, you can post presentations that you've made to your clients, position papers that you have written, pages of links to resources on the Web for topics of interest to you and your specialty, or even photographs of you and your staff. I have even used a website to post drafts of documents that I wanted a collaborator to review. The potential uses will become apparent, and, once you have the capability, you'll wonder how you ever got along without it.

Tips for Getting Up to Speed and Keeping Up with Developments

Despite the fact that keeping up with the constantly changing field of technological innovation may seem an impossible task, there are some simple steps that anyone can take to enhance his or her understanding of what is available and what is coming. The list that follows will point you in the right direction.

Recognize That Technological Innovations Warrant Your Attention. Even if you don't think of yourself as technically inclined, realize that developments in this field will impact your profession and therefore are as important for you to know about as are the developments in areas that you do consider more your specialty. So make it a point to read the articles on the Internet and technology that you see in major daily newspapers, such as *The New York Times* or *The Wall Street Journal,* or in weekly news magazines, such as *Time, Newsweek,* or *Business Week.* Once you get online, make it a point to check out technology news sections of sites like *The New York Times* technology section (www.nytimes.com/pages/technology/index.html) (requires a one-time free registration), CNET News (www.news.com), ZDNET

News (www.zdnet.com/zdnn/), or Wired News (www.wired.com). Just by glancing at headlines in these resources and reading the articles that capture your interest, you'll become acclimated to the latest developments and issues of interest to the networked world.

Go Online and Explore. Explore and experiment with using online tools like your browser, search engines, Usenet newsgroups, instant messaging programs, and Web page authoring programs to expand your understanding of and comfort with relying on them. You will learn more than you might expect just by spending time online. Save pages of interest to your "Favorites" folder in your browser (for Internet Explorer users) or "bookmark" them (if you happen to use Netscape or some other browser). You'll be able to revisit those sites when you need to, and the sites you've discovered during casual surfing may prove useful in a project for one of your clients. Your own interests and areas of expertise will, quite naturally and without special effort, help you to select the sites that will be most useful to you in your work.

Avail Yourself of Opportunities to Experience New Resources and Tools. Take opportunities to participate in online conferences as a participant, if those opportunities present themselves, so that you don't have the worry and responsibility for conducting the conference while you are learning. It is worthwhile to participate in a conference, even if the conference's topics do not seem to be of earth-shaking importance to you at the moment, just to have the experience of participating. You will find that you quickly learn about the dynamics of the conference, its limitations, and its strengths. As with anything, practice improves proficiency. When the time comes for you to use this online resource, you'll be better prepared for your leadership responsibilities.

Cultivate Relationships with Those Who Already Follow the Field. In almost anyone's circle of friends, there is at least one person who has become fascinated with the revolution that technology is making in society. Listening to these people talk about their interest can greatly improve your own familiarity with the field. While not everyone who talks a lot about the field is an expert, their comments can form the basis for further research or investigation. If you want to ask questions, find out how they became familiar with the field. Ask them what sites they find most useful in keeping up with changes in technology. Give them your e-mail address and invite them to send you links to sites that they think might help you get up to speed. This kind of person usually likes to share what he or she finds fascinating and won't mind becoming your mentor.

Subscribe to Mailing Lists That Provide Updates on Advances in Fields of Interest to You. Internet mailing lists provide information on almost every subject imaginable by sending e-mail to your address. Whether subscribing to newsletters about an application that you and your firm use, such as Microsoft Office, or about some other specific interest, such as utility deregulation, you become acclimated to a field quickly, even if you never post a question or comment. Just reading the comments and questions of others will quickly introduce you to the important issues.

And don't fear subscribing to an online newsletter. It is simply a matter of supplying your e-mail address to the list manager and perhaps replying to an introductory message (used primarily to validate your e-mail address) to start. Then you'll begin to receive the newsletter on the schedule that it is published (daily, weekly, monthly, or whenever). You can always unsubscribe if or when you decide the newsletter is no longer worth your time.

You can find a mailing list that matches your interests by visiting L-Soft's official catalog of lists at www.lsoft.com/lists/listref.html, where more than 52,380 public mailing lists are cataloged. (A much larger list of mailing lists is maintained, but not all of them are open to the public.) Just click on the "search" link and enter a keyword describing your interest.

Find an Opportunity to Attend a Technology Conference. Although these conferences, such as Comdex, are held regularly around the world and tend to be directed primarily to technology professionals, the average person can gain quite an appreciation of what is going on in the industry by visiting the exhibits and presentations. Comdex, for instance, occurs twice a year, in the spring and in the fall. Just walking through the acres of exhibits and listening to company representatives talk about their newly developed products will convey the sense of excitement and possibility that the industry generates. If attending such a conference is not possible, follow the reports of what is going on at them through one of the technology reporting sites such as CNET, ZDNET, or *Wired* magazine.

Join and Participate in an Online Interest Group. Many professional organizations like OD Network (see www.odnetwork.org) provide online venues for professionals in the field to meet and collaborate. Membership in some of these interest groups can provide opportunities to experience many of the innovations, such as online conferences, as a by-product of membership in the group. Other sites, such as www.fastcompany.com, www.tnbt.com, or even www.newedgeleadership.com, offer varying degrees of opportunity to participate with others interested in the effect the Internet will have on business. Joining one of these groups will give you access to others of like mind and the opportunity not just to learn but to contribute to the body of knowledge about how to use the Internet to your advantage in your consulting relationships.

Become Familiar with Usenet and Learn to Tap the Information It Contains. The Usenet consists of tens of thousands of newsgroups covering almost every subject imaginable. As such, it is a valuable resource, but a surprising number of people who are otherwise familiar with the Internet don't know much about it. Almost every subscription to an Internet service provider includes access to what is known as the "newsgroups." Yet, despite this fact, Usenet newsgroups remain an undiscovered resource for novice and even some experienced Internet users.

One reason that may account for this lack of use is that Usenet has the reputation in some circles for raucous and sometimes hostile exchanges that can go on for months or even years. Yet, amid this cacophony of diversity is a treasure trove of valuable information. Those who have the patience to learn to sort through these mountains of comments find these newsgroups to be just about the best source of help available for some subjects, such as how to use a particular software program.

A good place to start to learn about Usenet is at www.faqs.org/usenet/. This site will help to answer many questions that you may have about the process of profiting from the Usenet newsgroups. You'll also find helpful links to suggestions about etiquette on the newsgroups and ways to find the answers to your questions. Once you are ready to dive into the newsgroups, you can find a group that deals with your area of interest by visiting www.geocities.com/nnqweb/ngroups.html.

Accept the Fact That Something Fundamental Has Changed Because of the Networked World. While some might resist having to adapt to the new reality that the Internet and the advent of information technology have introduced, this reluctance to change will only perpetuate the difficulties of discovering the usefulness of these advances and delay the fun that being conversant with them brings. Resolve to jump into the middle of things, since there is no way to go backward and begin at the beginning. Take comfort in knowing that almost everyone else also had to begin in what appeared to be the middle too.

Most of us realize that it is our responsibility to read important new books or research that appears pertaining to our areas of expertise. The tools of the information age are just another of the components that we all will have to know and use. By establishing the habit of attending to the new developments in this field, you will be better prepared to help your clients as they adapt to the challenges of the 21st Century. Enjoy the challenge, and you'll be rewarded with increased skills as well as a lot of fun in the process. Good luck with your learning, because there is no end in sight.

Reference

Headlam, B. (2001, April 18). How to email like a CEO. *New York Times.* Copyright © 2001 by the New York Times Company. Reprinted by permission.

About the Author

In his thirty years of consulting experience, **Perry Nelson** *has often found himself in the position of doing something no one had done before. As the first consultant for Behavioral Systems, Inc., he developed the curriculum and pioneered the basic strategies that the company used as it applied behavioral psychology to its clients' needs. He was the company's first trainer for the consulting staff, which grew to over one hundred consultants. He was also the company's first area director and its first statewide supervisor.*

When his second consulting firm, Vernine and Associates, Inc., computerized its operations in the mid-1980s, he became the company authority on the use of the technology. He was the moving force behind the company's exploration and discovery of ways to integrate technology into its consulting operations with clients. Since retiring from consulting, he spends his time as a technical support agent for a large southeastern telecommunication company's DSL service, putting to use his interest in and knowledge of information technology to help resolve the customers' technical problems with the service.

9

HR and IT
Metamorphosis and Opportunities

Jana Markowitz

ON THE NEW ECONOMY, responsibilities and departmental organizations are beginning to blur. Technology's ubiquitous presence and use is driving change in traditional organization structures and responsibilities. HR and IT responsibilities in particular are beginning to overlap. The corporate structure of traditional organizations—manufacturers, distributors, retailers, and service providers—tends to be similarly composed of departments such as communications, marketing, human resources (HR), and information technology (IT), among others. All of these departments are meant to provide services for the entire organization, and each has clearly delineated responsibilities:

- Communications is responsible for press releases, public relations, and dealing with the media;

- Marketing is responsible for advertising and development of marketing programs;

- HR is responsible for recruiting, benefits, and compensation; and

- IT is responsible for telecommunication networks, computers, and the applications that run on them, ranging from centralized accounting to desktop applications such as e-mail and word processing.

But as technology becomes pervasive, the skills and structure needed to perform these functions are changing. To stay competitive, organizations must either develop new skills in traditional HR and IT departments or create entirely new departments and areas of responsibility to address the new needs. We will look at a variety of technology issues that are forcing changes in responsibilities, then review the options for changing organizations, people, and job descriptions to adapt to these and future technology-related challenges.

Technologies Begin to Blur the Lines

Specific technologies and their deployment—especially in new economy environments—are often responsible for the overlapping of departmental responsibilities. For example, in extranet (external website) deployments, the responsibilities of HR, marketing, communications, and IT overlap. HR may put recruiting information on the extranet, while marketing may be responsible for the look of the page, content on the home page (company history and so forth), and responding to questions and requests of site visitors. On the same extranet, communications may be responsible for online ads, press releases, and getting the site listed with various search engines. If the company's website also includes e-commerce capabilities with online transactions taking place (think of Amazon.com's website and the ability to order books), then an even wider variety of departments have responsibilities, including order entry, accounting, shipping, customer service, and so on.

Assigning responsibilities for extranets is actually one of the easier technology-related issues to resolve. Responsibilities can be clearly divided between the "content" of the site and the technology "mechanics" of enabling the site and keeping it available. The IT department (or an outsource vendor) can take responsibility for the technology mechanics, while leaving other internal departments responsible for content and responding to customer requests. Traditional organizational structures and job titles can work where the division of responsibilities regarding a technology is clear. IT can provide the technical platform, while other departments provide content and management of the information.

However, for the following technology applications, this sort of logical division of labor is not feasible:

- Telecommuting programs;
- E-learning (online training);
- Knowledge management; and
- Internet-based recruiting.

Let's review these technology-related areas to determine how organizational structures, job descriptions, and people need to change to adequately manage them.

Telecommuting

Telecommuting began approximately twenty years ago as a way to give computer programmers flexible hours and work environments. Telecommuting, sometimes called telework, can be broadly defined as the ability for an employee to perform work activities from a site other than company offices via the use of computers and network technology. Sometimes the worker is at home, but more often the worker is at a remote site either for a temporary project or to interact face-to-face with clients. The employee may be working from home, a hotel room, a satellite office, or a client's office, but in any case, he or she is not physically resident in the employer's facility.

An International Telework Association and Council (ITAC) survey indicates there were 16.5 million telecommuters in the United States in 2000 and predicts there will be 30 million workers telecommuting by the end of 2004.

As the business world moves to virtual teams, virtual companies, and geographically distributed work teams, and moves away from the "brick and mortar" environment of traditional organizations, telecommuting becomes a company-wide issue rather than an IT alternative-work option. While IT departments can provide laptop computers and network access for the worker, many business decisions need to take place before the telecommuter can become productive:

- How does the reporting process work? How often and by what medium (phone, e-mail, in person) does the employee report progress to his or her management? How is the person evaluated?

- What information and applications does the telecommuter need access to and at what times of day? (When can the IT group make applications unavailable to do maintenance work? Time zones and working at night complicate the answer to what should be a simple question.)

- How does departmental and peer communication work? (If the person is not in the office, how will he or she know what his or her cohorts are working on? How can the organization be sure business goals are aligned and that different groups are not working at cross-purposes?)

Rather than have each department try to develop these business rules, organizations should make these decisions in advance and develop policies and guidelines that they implement consistently across the company.

The International Telework Association and Council (ITAC) recommends that companies form a task force prior to implementing telecommuting to develop the company's telecommuting policies and guidelines. ITAC suggests that the following groups be represented on the task force:

- HR

- IT

- Legal

- Facilities planning

- Senior management

- Line supervisors

- Potential telecommuters

The Society for Human Resource Management (SHRM), a national organization for HR professionals, states in their "Telecommuting Position" that companies should provide written policies/guidelines on telecommuting to any employees, new or existing, who will be telecommuting. They also recommend that performance evaluation criteria be established in writing prior to beginning telecommuting and that evaluations be based on "objective and quantifying outcomes in relationship to defined goals."

Because telecommuting involves so much change to the traditional work environment and activities, organization development (OD) practitioners, internal or external, need to help establish the work processes and social norms for the physically absent telecommuters and their office cohorts and management.

Both HR and IT have substantial stakes in the outcome and ongoing activity of telecommuting, but there does not seem to be a clear definition of where overall accountability lies for telecommuting's success or failure. As neither HR nor IT has the full breadth of skills to plan and manage telecommuting, new departments (or positions) with appropriate cross-disciplinary skills are needed to take ongoing responsibility.

Telecommuting Information Internet Sites

www.telecommute.org (site of the International Telework Association and Council)

www.att.com/ehs/telecom.html (AT&T's Telework Guide)

www.inteleworks.com (Info on setting up a telecom program or starting to telecommute)

E-Learning

E-learning, also known as online training, is another area requiring both HR and IT skills. HR/Training departments have traditionally provided and tracked training. As more training becomes Internet-based or is delivered online, the skills needed to manage it are changing. IT may be better able to find, evaluate, and implement technology-delivered training, while HR may be better at deciding appropriate training content and assessing which employees need what training.

The American Society for Training and Development's (2001) *State of the Industry Report 2001* stated that in 1999, companies with more than 55,000 employees delivered 14 percent of formal training via e-learning. While this is still a small fraction of training, geographically distributed workers, lack of available time for training, and the cost of classroom delivery are likely to force the percentage of e-learning higher in all organizations. E-learning is still in its infancy, but its growth is expected to be phenomenal. W.R. Hambrecht and Company (2000), a well-known technology investment firm, projects that the business-to-business (corporate) online learning industry is expected to double in size each year until it reaches $11.5 billion in 2003.

E-learning differs from its predecessor, computer-based training (CBT), in several ways:

- Course material is generally located on a computer (server) other than the student's desktop (generally an intranet or Internet site);

- E-learning often involves interaction with an instructor or other students (per *Training* magazine's 1999 Industry Report, 36 percent of all training delivered online involves the student's interacting with other people online); and

- E-learning is usually linked to a learning management system.

A learning management system (LMS), according to *E-Learning Magazine,* provides the foundation for a corporate setting (Zielinski, 2000). An LMS helps corporations manage the administration, architecture, and reporting of learning activities. These systems include features such as:

- Database for tracking use, scores, proficiency;

- Registration facility;

- Curriculum and content management facility; and

- Means for delivering courses.

Some of the better-known learning management systems include Docent, Saba, and Click2Learn.

According to the American Society for Training and Development (Sanders, 2001), competencies needed to work with learning technologies include the traditional trainer skills and background, but also the following:

- Contracting skills;

- Awareness of the learning technology industry (current and emerging trends; limitations of current technologies; knowledge of the vendors; understanding the application of technologies to the learning environment);

- Management of learning technology evaluation and selection;

- Coordination skills for implementing and supporting learning technologies;

- Understanding of the effect of distributed method on learners; and

- Coordination skills for managing remote sites.

Although ASTD provides these competencies in its discussion of training professionals, many of the competencies are more reminiscent of IT employees, especially in the areas of technology evaluation, selection, and implementation management.

Neither traditional HR nor IT organizations are likely to have all of these competencies in their current staff. Either HR/training organizations must acquire new skills or new organizational structures and positions must be created.

Knowledge Management

According to Dr. Yogesh Malhotra, a noted author on knowledge management (KM), "Knowledge management focuses on 'doing the right thing' instead of 'doing things right.' In our thinking, knowledge management is a framework within which the organization views all its processes as knowledge processes. In this view, all business processes involve creation, dissemination, renewal, and application of knowledge toward organizational sustenance and survival" (Knowledge Management . . . , 1998).

Knowledge management systems have posed a problem to companies since their inception in the early 1980s. While individual departments and groups need to "own" content, the technical infrastructure clearly requires the skills of technologists. Getting individuals to agree to the "rules" for using these systems has also perpetually posed problems. To some people the perception that knowledge is power makes sharing that knowledge an undesirable activity, further complicating knowledge management implementation.

Knowledge management systems generally involve sharing of professional knowledge, for example, management consultants' sharing processes and working documents for helping clients manage areas of their business. The Big Five have used Lotus® Notes and other knowledge management systems to help their legions of consultants share information for many years. With the advent of intranets, a great deal of knowledge sharing began happening in a less structured, less managed environment.

Where does KM fit in an organization—the processes, the incentive systems to get employees to share, the updating of information to ensure it is accurate and current, the maintenance of the technical infrastructure? Although KM is technology-based, there are also many HR/OD skills needed to properly implement and manage KM.

E-Cruiting: Internet-Based Recruiting

E-cruiting seems on the surface to be a function of HR. After all, HR has been responsible for corporate recruiting since corporations were invented. But e-cruiting requires different skills than does traditional recruiting. To do Internet-based recruiting well requires a knowledge of the following:

- Where the job posting should go on the Internet to attract the right candidates;
- How to analyze massive numbers of online resumes (keywords may help or may cause you to toss out the best candidate); and

- How to use applicant tracking systems and videoconferencing to manage the candidate interview and selection processes.

Both technical skills and technology savvy are required to do Internet-based recruiting right, as major executive search firms discovered in developing their initial ventures into online recruiting.

According to Jim Quandt, COO and president of Heidrick & Struggles' Leaders! Online, e-cruiting differs from traditional search in scalability and timeliness. "Time-consuming steps in the recruiting cycle have been shortened via use of the Internet. . . . Leaders! has developed a unique 'opportunity site' where all the information about a position is viewed by a candidate once they have been matched. . . . This significantly reduces cycle time because the front-end qualifying and generation of candidate interest is done via technology" (*Interview with Jim Quandt*, 1999).

The online areas of executive search companies have specialists who use Web-based tools, as well as traditional methods, to identify and source candidates. The technically savvy staff are also responsible for getting targeted candidates to visit their websites and for developing content that will interest these candidates in adding their resumes and becoming frequent visitors.

Major search firms are rapidly developing e-cruiting capabilities, while most corporate HR organizations are content to list their jobs only on their company websites and in paper publications. This forces candidates to search out the company. As a result of many corporate HR departments taking too long to locate viable candidates and lacking the technical staff to recruit effectively online, many IT organizations have developed their own tech-recruiters internally and have taken the function away from HR. Companies not doing effective e-cruiting will lose the race for human capital and be unable to compete.

Approaches to HR/IT Integration

Several approaches are being used to handle the increasing number of overlapping responsibilities between IT and HR in the traditional organization structure:

- Create new job titles along with corresponding new areas of responsibility *or*

- Add new skills, responsibilities, and functions to existing organizations *or*

- Establish "special project" teams or task forces to address needs as they arise.

New Titles, Roles, and Areas of Responsibility

Many companies, traditional and new economy, are creating new job titles along with areas of responsibility to address the needs of new business processes and environments. Two executive jobs created in the 1990s are "chief learning officer" and "chief knowledge officer."

Chief Learning Officer

The chief learning officer (CLO) is usually responsible for all training—online and traditional—as well as assessing employees' skills and knowledge, maintaining skills databases, defining and providing professional development training, and providing "knowledge sharing" environments. Often, maintaining groupware and knowledge management systems becomes the CLO's organizational responsibility as well. This position usually reports to the CEO. In general, the person selected as a CLO has traditional HR/training background, but he or she also has a keen understanding of systems and emerging technologies as they relate to learning, training, and knowledge management. The author reviewed several Internet websites for job postings for CLOs or related positions. The following listings were found:

- E-learning manager
- Knowledge journalist
- Learning technologist
- Assistant learning manager
- Vice president, e-learning

Following are the minimum job requirements and position description for the vice president of e-learning position cited above:

Requirements

- Extensive knowledge and familiarity with e-learning capabilities, knowledge management systems, and Web-based applications;
- Exceptional project management skills;
- Strong change management skills;
- Strong client relationship skills;
- Strong business acumen;
- Strong communication skills;

- Highly motivated, self-starter; and
- Training and development/human resources background requested but not required.

Position Description

- Responsible for overall strategy, implementation, and management of the business unit's e-learning system;
- Reports to the director of learning and development;
- Responsible for the activities of technical manager for the e-learning initiative;
- Responsibilities include managing design and implementation of e-learning strategy; managing all e-learning content, including internal knowledge, learning modules, and external courseware; developing and maintaining content classification system (taxonomy); establishing and maintaining relationships with e-learning vendors; coordinating activities between division and company-wide e-learning strategies; assisting in developing and executing cultural change and incentive program; and acting as liaison to technology group to ensure technical infrastructure requirements and support.

It is clear that companies are seeking chief learning officers and other learning-related professionals with both training and technology skills to help the company adapt to the online learning and knowledge management needs of the new economy environment.

If a company's executive management places a high value on learning initiatives and professional development, OD practitioners should explore creating a new position and new department to focus on learning. This does not diminish the HR department, but rather frees them to provide more focused service in the areas of compensation and benefits.

Chief Knowledge Officer

The chief knowledge officer (CKO) has responsibility for implementing and maintaining knowledge management systems, which may include intranets, groupware, e-mail, and learning management systems. The terms chief learning officer and chief knowledge officer are often interchangeable, and their responsibilities are similar. However, the CKO position tends to require IT or systems background and is frequently aligned with IT, sometimes reporting to the CIO rather than the CEO. The author found the following job postings on BRINT, a business research Internet site with a job-posting area specifically for positions related to knowledge management:

- Chief knowledge officer (reporting to the CEO);
- CKO and chief technology officer (reporting to CFO);
- Manager of knowledge management systems (required fifteen years' IT experience); and
- Vice president of knowledge management (required ten years' senior consulting or technology experience, however, "technology background not a necessity").

Although CKOs tend to come from an IT background, they need strong people skills and the ability to forge good working relationships with the business users. Business departments depend on the CKO to be an intermediary for them, representing their interests to the IT organization, which provides the infrastructure needed to share information.

Buckman Labs

Buckman Labs is a company that has implemented both CLO and CKO positions, although they call their CLO a vice president of the Learning Center. Their experience, described below, illustrates some of the issues faced by organizations as they implement these new positions.

Buckman Labs is a small specialty chemicals company with approximately 1,350 employees headquartered in Memphis, Tennessee, but with a presence in twenty-two countries. Buckman Lab International provides "shared services" (IT, HR, finance, research and development, and training) for nineteen operating companies.

Well-managed and progressive, despite its tiny size, Buckman is able to take on chemical industry giants like DuPont and win. How is this possible? The corporate culture, according to Sheldon Ellis, vice president of the Buckman Labs Learning Center, values personal relationships and inspires a great deal of word-of-mouth knowledge exchange. This culture and knowledge-sharing environment is no accident; former CEO Bob Buckman (retired in Spring 2000 as CEO, but still leading the board of directors) started in the late 1980s to build a knowledge-sharing environment. He knew that the knowledge of his employees was his best competitive advantage, and that in countries where Buckman had few representatives, they needed to be able to draw on knowledge elsewhere in the company. That was why he established a chief knowledge officer (CKO) over the Knowledge Transfer Division (what traditionally would have been called IT) and later started a Learning Center—first as a special project, later adding the organizational structure to support it.

The Knowledge Transfer Division, under the CKO, maintains the technical infrastructure—servers, network, ERP systems, knowledge management systems, and other shared software—while the Learning Center provides systems training, professional development training, quality processes, and some performance consulting (organization development). Ellis, whose position is equivalent to a CLO and who reports to the CEO, implemented a learning management system, Click2Learn's Ingenium, which maintains records and administration for training. The Learning Center is also in the process of developing a skills database.

As the Learning Center organization was built, it picked up several Buckman Knowledge Transfer Division (IT) workers who had experience with Lotus® Notes/ Domino-based knowledge management systems. In addition, the Learning Center added people with OD and adult learning backgrounds. The vice president of the Learning Center has neither IT nor HR background, but came from the sales side of the company, with a strong field reputation for project management.

In building the Learning Center, Ellis had the complete backing of both the CEO and the entire executive team. What he did not have was time. The executives wanted a prototype for the Learning Center delivered three weeks after Ellis's start date. While he delivered this prototype on time, in retrospect he would have preferred to get input and buy-in from the field and from middle management. These people, as the users and targets of change, were surprised and somewhat resistant during implementation simply because they had been left out of the loop in the quick start of the Learning Center.

Asked whether the Buckman Labs organization structure with a CKO and CLO was successful in supporting knowledge management and e-learning, Ellis replied that everything in the company was based on knowledge management and that KM was not tied to a particular department but was part of the culture, infrastructure, and employee attitude. Buckman Labs attributes its success as a company to its culture, which encourages proactive sharing of knowledge.

Were HR or the Knowledge Transfer Division jealous of the Learning Center's taking over some organization development and technical responsibilities from their respective areas? Ellis indicated that both departments felt the Learning Center added to and complemented their work, rather than diminishing it.

Does Ellis think dot-coms require a different organization structure than traditional corporations? In responding, Ellis indicated that the distinction between traditional and dot-com organizations is blurring quickly. Both types of companies have an increasing reliance on technology and customers pushing them for speed and customization. This means an employee needs to use discretionary time for the company (nights, weekends, whatever is called for), and in turn the company must invest in the capability of the employee—training, professional development, whatever gives the employee better skills and the sense that he or she is valued. Providing the employee access to the company's breadth of knowledge is also critical. Ellis does not see how Buckman Labs could be successful against competitors without its knowledge management and learning center concepts. Of significant importance, the CEO did not believe they could do without these entities either.

For change leaders and consultants proposing to set up CLO or CKO positions with accompanying staff, it is clearly a critical success factor to have the CEO and upper echelon of management backing the initiative and the new executives. In isolation from the operations of the business, a CLO/CKO position will become meaningless and be eliminated in the next reorganization.

Another key to successfully establishing CLO/CKO positions is to plan their roles and functions carefully, not damaging existing HR and IT organizations or raiding their staff. Of course, change leaders and consultants also know that getting the involvement of the change targets is equally critical in launching a successful new department. Buckman was fortunate in being able to address the resistance brought by lack of buy-in.

New Skills and Responsibilities in the Existing Organization

For companies that do not have the luxury of creating new departments, functions, and job titles, there is the option of expanding skills and responsibilities within the existing organizational structure.

Some IT organizations are recognizing a need to add staff with organization development skills, training background, and HR background. The staff with OD/HR background is put to work fostering collaborative work relationships with other departments, as well as supporting intranet/extranet, telecommuting, and e-cruiting activities. In addition, these people oversee e-learning programs and IT professional development and perform IT strategic planning. In other words, IT creates a mini-HR/OD department within itself to support its needs and relationships with the rest of the organization.

HR may do something very similar, staffing itself with people who have technology backgrounds to implement and run their HRIS (human resource information systems), manage e-learning (Internet-based training), and maintain intranet information.

In some cases, the same company may have people with an HR background working in the IT department and people with an IT background on staff in HR. Without a new organization or new job titles for these overlapping responsibilities, each traditional organization has to expand existing positions to meet its needs.

HR and IT departments in many companies are not on good terms—each feeling the other is giving it poor service. HR frequently feels its systems and technology needs are receiving low priority. IT fumes over technical positions that remain open for months with few, if any, viable candidates offered by HR. Introducing HR-background staff into IT and vice versa can prove frustrating and difficult for the individual trying to fit in.

Selecting and preparing employees for this crossover work is similar to preparing an employee for a foreign assignment. The culture, terminology, and expectations in HR and IT departments are very different, their common corporate culture notwithstanding. Making the career path clear to the employee and providing an understanding of the value of multidisciplinary skills is also important.

As these additions in IT and HR become more visible to top executives, the opportunity, and need, to create a CKO or CLO position and associated department may become apparent. If learning management systems are being run by "techies" in HR and e-cruiting is the responsibility of IT staff, internal change leaders and consultants should evaluate the need to update the organizational structure and job descriptions. If the business need is clear, change leaders and consultants should raise the issue with executive management. However, if issues of overlapping function in IT and HR are not even on the horizon, changing the structure without a driving business need could prove disastrous. Timing, business need, and executive support are all crucial to such organizational structure changes.

Special Project Teams and Multifunctional Teams

Some organizations must adhere strictly to their existing job descriptions, responsibilities, and organizational structure. How then do they implement knowledge management, telecommuting, and e-learning? They use the traditional approach of project teams—pulling the necessary skills from wherever in the organization they exist: technical skills from IT, facilitation skills from HR, business process skills from business departments, and so forth.

This actually works well for implementation of new technologies and new processes because it pulls the right expertise together as a single, goal-oriented team. It is the approach used by Big Five consulting firms when they implement enterprise resource planning (ERP) systems such as SAP, Baan, and PeopleSoft. ERP systems require adjustments to business processes as well as technology implementation and changes in departmental relationships. Because ERP implementations are such vast undertakings, frequently lasting two to three years, and impact so much of the organization, the project teams become semi-permanent entities made up of both employees and consultants. Where this can fall apart is in the ongoing management of the new system or process after the project is complete. Once the project ends and the team disbands, there have to be very clearly defined responsibilities and accountabilities for sustaining the new system, processes, and functions. Without an organizational structure in place to "own" the new system and processes, this approach can easily fail.

Buckman Labs used a project approach successfully in implementing their Learning Center. The initial entity was created quickly by a project team, but a subsequent organizational structure was put in place, including permanent staff with appropriate skills and a vice president (CLO) over the area who reports to the CEO.

Should a New Economy Company Even Have an IT Organization?

Many articles have been written over the last five years predicting the end of IT organizations as we know them today. As much IT infrastructure work is outsourced, many futurists predict that all technology work will be provided to new economy companies by ESPs (external service providers, outsourcers), ASPs (application service providers), and ISPs (Internet service providers). In combination, these three types of providers can give a company technical infrastructure; application installation, management, and support; and Internet access for e-mail, research, and other network-centric work.

What these articles do not take into account is that many companies will want to develop technology-based competitive advantages (again think of Amazon.com and their leapfrogging ahead of other booksellers) and will not want these created by an outside vendor who can also sell them to a competitor.

The traditional IT department that provides all technology-related services for a huge corporation may, indeed, become a thing of the past over the next ten years, but there will still be an IT department that provides innovative technologies, evaluates emerging technologies, and supports advanced technologies. This is *not* your father's IT. The new IT worker is a hybrid professional with vendor management skills (to manage the providers of outsourced services), business acumen, change management skills, and a variety of other abilities in addition to his or her technology savvy. While few of these hybrid professionals exist today, organizations are building them through experience and education as quickly as possible.

Outside the IT department, business managers will need to have a deeper understanding of technologies and technology-related issues in their areas of business. The need for hybrid workers with both technical and business acumen is increasing as rapidly outside IT as inside.

In future IT departments, the CIO (chief information officer) may work in conjunction with a CKO (chief knowledge officer) and CTO (chief technology officer). The CIO job is evolving into a strategic-planning and business-visioning position, while day-to-day technology operations will fall to the CTO. Providing business users with access to information-gathering and information-sharing environments will fall to the CKO. This is definitely not the traditional IT organization, nor for that matter will other departments remain unchanged. New economy and traditional organizations alike are having to evolve to deal with the new realities that the Internet and emerging technologies are forcing on them.

Conclusion

Traditional HR and IT organizations may, in the future, be limited in function—compensation and benefits for HR, technology infrastructure (hardware, software, networks) for IT. New departments may handle technology initiatives that require multidisciplinary skills—telecommuting, knowledge management, e-learning, and e-cruiting. Envisioning these new departments and "hybrid" employees with IT, HR, and business skills, the OD practitioner will also see opportunities.

Internal change leaders and consultants may be able to offer employees career paths that cross several functional areas—including HR, IT, and business operations. The "hybrid" employees will in turn provide a rich pool of executive candidates as they will have both contacts and experience in several areas of the organization. In defining professional development for business people, change leaders and consultants should offer IT professionals "soft skills" such as vendor relationship management, negotiating, and facilitation. Similarly, business and HR professionals should be offered technology updates to keep them abreast of technical trends in their areas.

External change leaders and consultants will see opportunities to provide HR/OD services to IT organizations that are not able to build HR skills internally and do not have HR departments with IT-specific skills. Gartner Group, a well-known market research and consulting firm specializing in the IT industry, recently started a subsidiary, people[3], which is focused on providing HR services to IT clients. People[3]'s consultants have both IT and HR expertise and are careful to involve both the HR and IT departments in their engagements. Services that IT clients are requesting include compensation studies, assistance in developing IT career paths, and software that provides a skills database and aids in selecting people with appropriate skills for project teams.

The driving role of technology in every area of business means that change leaders and consultants will have to work quickly to develop the "hybrid" employees and executives that corporations are already seeking—those with business acumen, technology awareness, and extensive communication and change management skills. Internal and external change leaders and consultants will find ample opportunity to provide new organizational structures, professional development, and new career paths to produce multidisciplinary professionals and executives.

References

American Society for Training and Development. (2001, March). *State of the industry report 2001* [online]. Available:www.astd.org/members/research/2001_state_of_the_industry_full_report.pdf [member access only]

Interview with Jim Quandt, chief operating officer, LeadersOnline. (1999). Press release [online]. Available: www.leadersonline.com/pressroom.asp?file=jq_interview.html

Knowledge management, knowledge organizations and knowledge workers: A view from the front lines. (1998, February 19). *Maeil Business News* (Korea) [online]. Available: www.brint.com/interview/maeil.htm

Sanders, E.S. (2001, March). E-learning competencies. *Learning Circuits* [online]. Available: www.learningcircuits.com [To access this article, under "Archive" in the right-hand column on the home page, click on "Learning Circuits." When the search page appears, enter "2001" for year and "Sanders" for author.]

W.R. Hambrecht & Co. (2000, April). *Industry report: E-learning: Exploring a new frontier* [online]. Available: www.wrhambrecht.com/research/elearning/ir/index.html

Zielinski, R. (2000, October). Online 101: Can anyone tell me what an LMS is? *E-learning Magazine* [online]. Available: www.elearningmag.com/issues/ Oct00/online.asp

1999 Industry Report. (1999, October). *Training* [online]. Available: www.training-supersite.com/publications/archive/training/1999/910/910cv.htm

About the Author

Jana Markowitz *is the founder of The Collective Mind, a consulting firm specializing in OD services (facilitation, strategic planning, management seminars, and executive coaching) for information technology clients. Her background includes a bachelor's degree in computer science from Vanderbilt University, fifteen years' technology consulting experience at IBM, a master's degree in organizational psychology, and seven years of management consulting experience. She is a qualified Myers-Briggs trainer and a member of the following professional organizations: American Society for Training and Development (ASTD), the Organization Development Network (ODN), Society for Information Management (SIM), and Society for Human Resource Management (SHRM). She can be reached via email at jmarkowitz@mindspring.com.*

Part 5

Conclusions and Implications

ⒺARLY IN THIS BOOK we observed that technology change forces change in the way societies organize themselves, and that in turn forces changes in the premises, values, and even the thought processes of people. That has been true since the earliest days of mankind with the invention of agriculture and is the case today with the effects of information technology. In the preceding chapters we have identified derived imperatives of technological change:

- The ability to respond to unforeseeable change replaces prediction and control as key skills;

- People substitute Internet interaction for face-to-face interaction; and

- Conventional jobs abruptly require entirely new and unrelated skill sets in order to perform them competently.

Taking these imperatives cumulatively, we may well be living in an era in which discontinuous change (rather than gradual change) has become the norm. Our final chapter examines the relationship of continually emerging changes in organizations to some parallel changes in today's larger society. It invites the reader to consider some points of view he or she may not have considered before.

Re-Evaluating Our Values for a Better Fit

Stan Herman

PERHAPS NOWHERE ELSE is the derived imperative of discontinuous change more fundamentally illustrated than in its effect on organization cultures. We are in the midst of a new paradigm that is forming around us—a paradigm that brings with it a markedly different notion about the nature of reality in organizations and how reality is formed and re-formed. Let us note immediately that, in speaking about the nature of reality, we are not theorizing about an abstract philosophical formulation; we are talking about how we address the process of planning, prioritizing, and performing work.

In this concluding chapter, I will attempt to look at some of the social and psychological consequences of the networked economy, particularly with respect to values and the emergence of new theories and movements affecting organization and leadership worldviews.

The subject of "values" has been dealt with in the past almost invariably as an abstract and wispy one. Our values have, by and large, been expressed as ideals—behavior to be aspired toward (but seldom if ever reached)—rather than as "ground level" descriptions of the patterns of our actual behavior. I believe that in the networked economy this posture is no longer suitable. We are in an era of hyper-sophistication. With exposure to the Internet, with opportunity to communicate at almost instant speed with others, literally around the globe, to have access to the perspectives of different cultures, critiques, and "exposés" from all points on the political spectrum, we are among the most skeptical (some say "cynical") generation in living memory. It is a generation that pays scant attention to high-sounding abstractions.

In the interests of climbing down the abstraction ladder a step or two, let's start by distinguishing simply between two varieties of values: "ideal" values and "operational" values. Ideal values are those we conceive as "good" and espouse to others. Operational values are the choices of behavior we actually make. We know them by looking back over our shoulders at what we have just done. It is important to keep ideal values and operational values reasonably close. If they are not, ideal values tend to become little more than slogans with scant credibility. For example, organizations that had long proclaimed in their "vision" statements that they believed their employees to be their "most important resources" lost credibility when they initiated large-scale downsizing exercises. It became clear that competitiveness (or stock performance) was a considerably more important *operational* value.

Those charged with organization leadership, as well as the consultants who support them, will need to recognize and define new balance points that better and more authentically describe the sometimes countervailing interests of the organization and the individual, as well as the organization and the society. This is especially true for younger generation knowledge workers who are highly skeptical of the "usual b.s.," as one I know puts it.

Ideal Values

A few years ago, Warner Burke, a senior management consultant and professor of organization behavior at Columbia Teachers College, identified [ideal] core values of the organization development field (see Drucker, 1999). Most prominently these included human development, fairness, choice, openness, and balance of autonomy and constraint in management. While discussions of values are notoriously fraught with controversy in most fields, Burke's list is probably the one most agreed to among at least those consultants who have any concern about the subject of values at all. I am indebted to him for his generous permission to use his list as a "take-off" point.

Following is a summary description of each of his five, followed by what we believe to be important modifications required by the new economy.

Human Development: Full Realization of Individual Potential. The organization can no longer be looked to as a dependable provider of initiative in this area. It may be very generous in times of high profits, but unless compelled by government regulations or an employment contract, the generosity will disappear in times of tight competition. The "social compact" of the past, in which employees offered loyalty and good work in exchange for secure employment and a chance to rise in the organization hierarchy, is no more. Some companies will provide training opportunities that are directly useful for their current or near-term foreseeable business needs, but are likely to provide this only when the labor market makes that advantageous (over the option of using less costly outside sources). I believe that a realistic requirement for human development in this uncertain environment is a renewed focus on the *individual* and his or her capacity to adapt and establish himself or herself in new settings. Training ought to be provided both in schools and in entry-level jobs that develop skills in both collaboration and taking care of one's legitimate self-interests.

Fairness and Choice. People in organizations should be treated equitably without discrimination, with dignity, and be free from coercion. The increase in highly skilled knowledge workers and the complexity of their work discourages coercion and arbitrariness, especially during worker shortages. Federal and state legislation have accomplished a great deal to outlaw discrimination. Employment contracts have long been a feature of executive employment. Contracts are also a feature when companies outsource project work. It may be that our best assurance of "fairness" lies in making employment contracts available to all knowledge workers (and perhaps eventually to all employees).

At the same time, it must be noted that ideas of "fairness" change with the times and generations. The "social compact" of two or three decades ago that we spoke of above is clearly gone. Now, even companies that are highly profitable "re-engineer" and downsize. In a recent experience of the author working with a large group of people who had been downsized, I discovered, to my surprise, that they accepted the action matter-of-factly and with almost no resentment. While "employment security" had been a highly prized value for their parents, it was not for this group, who fully expected to change companies and careers many times during their work lives.

Today's workers expect little security from and feel little loyalty to their organizations. Unlike their parents or in some cases grandparents, they have not experienced much involuntary unemployment or the threat of poverty. Many are more focused on what some see as unrelieved acquisitiveness. As Jay Whitehead, of EmployeeService.com, put it in a NewsHour interview, "There [is] a real downside to the lifestyle that the Internet economy has thrown upon a lot of the workers. You've got people who are working sixteen, eighteen, nineteen hours a day for weeks, months, quarters, and even years on end to reach horrendous financial heights. People really are looking to their jobs for their entire personal life. In fact, there's a term in Silicon Valley for the lack of a personal life, a sex life. [It's] called Internet Interruptus."

Openness. This defines communication in organizations conducted with forthrightness, honesty, and integrity. Information technology strongly favors openness in what information technology labels "transparency." Not because the organization necessarily holds either honesty or integrity as a value, but because the free exchange of technical and business information is required for swift decision making and action.

Once this kind of interchange becomes the norm, possibilities for increasing candor and authenticity in other areas may become more likely. But they may require changes in common practice that can conflict with political correctness.

"Cluetrain," a group of internet technologists and philosophers of the new economy, consider that the Internet itself is forcing power sharing in organizations. According to Cluetrain, " Hyperlinks subvert hierarchy . . . [and] networked conversations are enabling powerful new forms of social organization and knowledge exchange to emerge" (Locke, Levine, Searls, & Weinberger, 2000).

Balance of Autonomy and Constraint. Workers should have the freedom to perform their work as they see fit within reasonable organizational constraints. As we have said, many workers will be geographically dispersed and working more independently than ever before. Conventional performance appraisal and merit pay systems won't work in virtual environments. Questions for organizations about when and how to impose controls on Internet surfing, personal e-mails, and other "nonproductive" activities present difficult dilemmas: When do restrictions inhibit creativity and breed costly resentment? How does a "monitor" distinguish non-productive effort?

New Theories

When we talk about values, we need to recognize that particular ideas of goodness and badness are based on some fundamental cultural assumptions. For example, in contemporary American society, physical aggression and violence are clearly seen as "bad," but in the Japanese Bushido culture—the code of samurai warriors—it is seen as a set of positive qualities. Many of the values North Americans now espouse, with respect, for example, to gender roles and sexual practices, have changed dramatically over the last several decades. Therefore it will be useful to also examine some of the fundamental premises and concepts emerging in our era—spirituality, complexity theory, and post-modernism—to see whether we can determine the source of some of our values "mutations."

Spirituality

Spirituality in organizations appears in two forms: sectarian—for example, "Born Again" Christianity—and universal—a general, nondenominational communion with a superior or transcendent state of goodness. Neither of these is really new to the organization scene. Since the beginning of the industrial age, many employers have introduced Christian movements into their companies (for example, JC Penney). A few in the United States have introduced other religions as well.

What is relatively recent is the introduction of "New Science"-based explanations and legitimations of the higher levels of human consciousness. Even before new science though, about three decades ago, a field called "Organization Transformation" was supported by theories from subatomic physics and eastern metaphysics—including Buddhism, Hinduism, and the Tao.

For many, the center of nonsectarian spirituality is "values based" and humanistic. The main messages have to do with such things as preserving our planet and its creatures, the expansion of participative democratic principles and practices into the workplace, building better communities, and so forth.

To some people, nonsectarian spirituality closely resembles what a previous generation called "secular humanism"—with its concentration on good rather than

God and reason rather than faith. Thus, to some, it may seem too exclusively "earthbound" in its concerns to really be called spiritual. But there are elements of the new sciences—especially complexity (and chaos) theory—that can take us beyond "left-brain" linear logic and introduce us, if not to God, then to a point of view that transcends ordinary thinking.

Complexity and Chaos Theory

One of the most intriguing aspects of these new economy times for me are the speculations about "complexity theory" (often identified with "chaos theory") and the remarkably close relationships of many of its tenets with the physics and economics of information technology. Complexity theory fits right in with the premises of a number of the best-known information technologists and theoreticians in their fields.

According to Jonathan Rosenhead (2001),* in a paper appearing in the journal *Science as Culture*, "The more general name for the field is complexity theory (within which 'chaos' is a particular mode of behavior). Complexity theory is concerned with the behavior over time of certain kinds of complex systems. These range as widely as astronomy, chemistry, evolutionary biology, geology and meteorology." Rosenhead uses the work of Ralph Stacey (1992), an organization consultant, and others to point out the key relevance of complexity theory for managers. Basically, it is that the future is unknowable. Therefore, "The common assumption among managers," says Stacey (1992), "that part of their job is to decide where the organization is going and to take decisions designed to get it there is seen as a dangerous delusion."

Because of this "fact," such conventional processes as statistical analysis, forecasting, and long-range planning are limited in their usefulness. Since no two situations are ever identical, analytical reviews of the past as a basis for future planning will usually be faulty. Similarly, "visioning" becomes an exercise in "illusions," since a consensual vision of the organization in five years is bound to be wrong. Perhaps most disturbing of all to many consultants, according to Stacey, a strong common culture becomes not an advantage but a serious limitation because "the dynamics of 'group think'. . . are potent pressures for conformity. This is not an atmosphere in which searching re-examination of cherished assumptions can thrive. Rather than trying to consolidate stable equilibrium, the organization should aim to position itself in *a region of bounded instability*" (Stacey, 1992).

---

*Reprinted with the permission of the publisher. From *Complexity Theory and Management Practice*, copyright © 2001 by J. Rosenhead, Berrett-Koehler Publishers, Inc., San Francisco, CA. All rights reserved. 1-800-929-2929.

After our immersion in the cold waters of complexity theory's implications for organizations, we also ought to note that neither Rosenhead nor Stacey wants to throw out current management orthodoxy altogether. Stacey sees the need for "ordinary" (orthodox) management and "extraordinary" management. He says, "Ordinary management is required in order to carry out day-to-day problem solving to achieve the organization's established objectives. It employs a logical analytic process involving data analysis, goal setting, evaluating options against goals, rational choice, implementation through the hierarchy, and monitoring. This is planning and management based on a shared ideological consensus, with control at its centres. Competent ordinary management is necessary if the organisation is to deliver cost-effective performance. Extraordinary management, by contrast, is what is required if the organisation is to be able to transform itself in situations of open-ended change" (Stacey, 1992). Stacey acknowledges that both ordinary and extraordinary management are needed. Rosenhead (1992) points out, "There is, however, an intrinsic tension between the two modes." And, I would add, one of the highest skills required of top management is the dynamic balancing of such tension.

Finally, Rosenhead cautions wisely that those of us involved in the study and practices of organization management ought not take complexity theory applied to organizations as revealing literal truth. First, complexity theory is a relatively new field and has not, even in the natural sciences, developed a unified body of thought. Second, there is no good reason to assume that discoveries applicable to the natural sciences also necessarily apply to social processes. He suggests that complexity theory can serve us best if we think of it as metaphor rather than as scientific facts about society. This writer agrees and would add that a good metaphor, like a good model, should tell us where to look, not what to see.

We are speaking here of new models, and they are in large part "nonmodels"; they leave you up in the air with nothing solid or familiar to pin yourself to. Dealing with a new nonmodel is often neither easy nor pleasant. Bradford Koening, investment banker of Goldman Sachs, has observed five stages that a typical old economy organization goes through as it notices a new economy competitor and confronts the nonmodel of the new economy:

1. *Ridicule:* "What a lousy way to make money."

2. *Bemusement:* "How interesting that everyone's paying so much attention to such a small operation."

3. *Recognition:* "Wow, they're growing quickly."

4. *Fear:* "That eighteen-month-old company is taking share from us."

5. *Panic:* "I'll be out of a job it I don't get a Net strategy soon."

Post-Modernism

Let's now consider the third and, probably for the usual business reader, "farthest out" element of our triumvirate, post-modernism.

As theorists see it, the new economy is contributing to a new post-modern society that its advocates say requires new concepts and theories. Some, like Fredric Jameson and David Harvey interpret the post-modern as "a higher stage of capitalism marked by a greater degree of capital penetration and homogenization across the globe." The globalization of business and the widespread availability of venture capital to new start-ups (until recently) would seem to support this. These processes are also producing "increased cultural fragmentation, changes in the experience of space and time, and new modes of experience, subjectivity, and culture." (Quotes are from Web sources, now unavailable.)

Increasing cultural fragmentation is recognizable in the rapid growth of special interest groups in all parts of our society from professional societies through lobbying groups to ethnic, "disadvantaged," and sexual preference groups. Most of these segments of the general society are catered to by specialized television channels and websites that span the subject matter of the known universe. While we may be a bit premature, it is not hard to predict that the increasing development of virtual reality technology probably will (if it does not already) offer changes in the experience of space and time for those who immerse themselves in participation.

For post-modernists, conventional ways of formulating theories are seen as faulty because those who formulate them insist on trying to establish invariable principles that account for all conditions. Post-modern thinkers do not believe that is either possible or useful, and they believe that those who attempt to espouse such theories often rationalize and ignore exceptions in order to make their case.

In the organization and management field, we can see the expression of this fault in the continual attempts of "experts" to specify the "one best" and truest model and prescription for organizing and managing. But as Peter Drucker (1999) has said on many occasions (and an increasing number of authorities are agreeing), "The executive of the future will require a toolbox full of organizational structures. He will have to select the right tool for each specific task. That means he or she will have to learn to use each of the tools and understand which one works best for each task. And when, in the performance of a task, should he or she switch from one kind of organization to another?"

Defenders of "modern" theory, by contrast, attack post-modernism as relativistic, irrational, and nihilistic. Post-modern theorists don't argue this. They say that the "modern" belief that theory mirrors reality is incorrect. For them what you see depends on *where you view it from* and *what you are looking for.* Theories, at best, provide partial perspectives on their objects and are always influenced by the history and language of a culture. If your culture and language (as is the case in some Native American cultures) has a counting system that can only stipulate 1, 2, 3, and "many," you are not likely to theorize about higher mathematics and science as we know them. If, on the other hand, you live in contemporary American culture, you are not likely to notice or linguistically distinguish among the scores of varieties of snow, which many Eskimo societies recognize. All of these observations are clearly applicable within individual organizations as well as in society as a whole. Their implications, I believe, are profound. As many, perhaps most, of the senior-level executives I have worked with over the years have admitted to me in private, their use for and observation of management theory in their day-to-day operating choices and decisions very often give way to their hunches and intuitions. The influences of past history, cultural patterns, and established routines very often determine the "boxes" within which an organization will look for solutions to its problems or opportunities for its future. Traditional managers in old-line, basic manufacturing organizations are less likely to give much attention to leading-edge technology—or place high value on its use—than are young managers in the Silicon Valley.

Post-modernists believe that *microtheories* and *micropolitics* (theories and interactions that apply to a limited situation or case at a given point in time) better reflect reality and are more useful. The people of the *Information Age* are less dependent on having normalized and regularized structures, models, and procedures than those of the *Industrial Age.* They expect more ambiguity in their lives and are better able to live with that ambiguity. Note that they, too, require some structure, but, in general, a whole lot less than their predecessors did. Fewer of them become "true believers" in a particular theoretical model of the one best way to organize or operate. Pragmatism—choosing your best guess/estimate of what will work in a given situation—is their preferred style.

Helpful or Heretical?

For many in our society, the ideas of chaos and a less controllable future are the very antithesis of what organizations ought to be about. As one colleague said, "We do need to have something firm to hold on to—some certainties with which to respond to others and more importantly to ourselves. That's been what science and logical reasoning have been about since the age of the enlightenment."

To which the post-modernist and complexity champions might respond, "Neither you nor I, nor any other thinking being, ever has had something firm. All we have is the nonfirm—temporary theories and practices that, as has always been true in the past, will eventually be replaced." As Bill Gates (1999) wrote, "Punctuated chaos rather than punctuated equilibrium" is now the rule.

Expanding and Extending Perspectives

Earlier we noted Bradford Koening's five stages of response to new economy realities: ridicule, bemusement, recognition, fear, and panic. A somewhat more optimistic alternative is the following, to which we subscribe:

A Human Reaction Cycle

1. Deny and resist radical change;

2. Accept and adapt to it;

3. Prepare for it; and then

4. Lead it.

As we have seen, the changes in new economy organizations are considerable. The impact of their *derived imperatives* on management and leadership (and consulting) has turned some of our most cherished premises upside down. Dealing with these changes will require openness to new possibilities and learning new skills. More and more of us will find ourselves expanding our perspectives by developing our abilities to recognize increasing numbers and varieties of others' viewpoints. We will also discover that, as we expand our perspectives, we can also extend them by allowing ourselves to access our inner wisdoms that reveal the source of all perspectives. The implications of these shifts require us to re-examine some of our fundamental premises and perhaps to re-invent not only organizations but ourselves as well. We who have written for this book hope that it will contribute to the re-invention process.

References

Drucker, P. (1999). *Management challenges for the 21st century.* New York: Harper-Business.

Gates, B. (1999). *Business at the speed of thought.* New York: Warner.

Locke, C., Levine, R., Searls, R., & Weinberger, D. (2000). *The cluetrain manifesto: The end of business as usual.* Cambridge, MA: Perseus.

Mitleton-Kelly, E. (1997). *Organisations as co-evolving complex adaptive systems* [BPRC Paper No. 5]. Business Process Resource Centre, University of Warwick, Coventry.

Rosenhead, J. (1992). Into the swamp: The analysis of social issues. *Journal of the Operational Research Society, 43,* 293–305.

Rosenhead, J. (2001). Complexity theory and management practice. [on-line]. Available: www.human-nature.com/science-as-culture/rosenhead.html

Senge, P.M. (1990). *The fifth discipline: The art and practice of the learning organization.* New York: Doubleday.

Stacey, R.D. (1992). *Managing the unknowable: Strategic boundaries between order and chaos in organizations.* San Francisco: Jossey-Bass.

Von Krogh, G., Ichijo, K., & Nonaka, I. (2000). *Enabling knowledge creation.* New York: Oxford University Press.

About the Editor

Stan **Herman** has more than thirty years of experience as an internal manager (GE and TRW) and external consultant working with senior and middle management of Fortune 200 (and some smaller) companies. His focus is on coaching and counseling executives; planning and implementing highly focused, "situation-specific" improvement efforts; large-scale change; team assessment and development; and other organization issues related to networked and new economy work groups.

Mr. Herman is the author of four previous books and has also written more than one hundred articles and columns published in professional journals, popular magazines, the business press, and general newspapers. Two books have been adapted as videos. He has instructed at a number of universities, including the University of Southern California, the University of California at Los Angeles, the University of Richmond, the University of Wisconsin, and Pepperdine University, as well as teaching at the University Associates Intern program. His work has been featured in audiotapes, and he has been a guest on many radio talk shows.

His primary current interest is in identifying shifts in organization process and structures required by the networked economy and in redesigning management and consulting approaches for effective responses. Accessing personal spirit and developing its practical applications in contemporary organizations is another area of particular interest.

Mr. Herman can be contacted by phone at 760-480-1628 or by e-mail at SMHerman @aol.com.

About the
Series Editors

William J. Rothwell, Ph.D., is president of Rothwell and Associates, a private consulting firm, as well as professor of human resources development on the University Park Campus of The Pennsylvania State University. Before arriving at Penn State in 1993, he was an assistant vice president and management development director for a major insurance company and a training director in a state government agency. He has worked full-time in human resources management and employee training and development from 1979 to the present. He thus combines real-world experience with academic and consulting experience. As a consultant, Dr. Rothwell's client list includes over thirty-five companies from the Fortune 500.

Dr. Rothwell received his Ph.D. with a specialization in employee training from the University of Illinois at Urbana-Champaign, his M.B.A. with a specialization in human resources management from Sangamon State University (now called the

University of Illinois at Springfield), his M.A. from the University of Illinois at Urbana-Champaign, and his B.A. from Illinois State University. He holds lifetime accreditation as a Senior Professional in Human Resources (SPHR), has been accredited as a Registered Organization Development Consultant (RODC), and holds the industry designation as Fellow of the Life Management Institute (FLMI).

Dr. Rothwell's latest publications include *The Manager and Change Leader* (ASTD, 2001); *The Role of Intervention Selector, Designer and Developer, and Implementor* (ASTD, 2000); *ASTD Models for Human Performance* (2nd ed.) (ASTD, 2000); *The Analyst* (ASTD, 2000); *The Evaluator* (ASTD, 2000); *The ASTD Reference Guide to Workplace Learning and Performance* (3rd ed.), with H. Sredl (HRD Press, 2000); *The Complete Guide to Training Delivery: A Competency-Based Approach,* with S. King and M. King (AMACOM, 2000); *Human Performance Improvement: Building Practitioner Competence,* with C. Hohne and S. King (Butterworth-Heinemann, 2000); *Effective Succession Planning: Ensuring Leadership Continuity and Building Talent from Within* (2nd ed.) (AMACOM, 2000); and *The Competency Toolkit,* with D. Dubois (HRD Press, 2000).

Roland Sullivan, RODC, has worked as an OD pioneer with nearly eight hundred systems in eleven countries and virtually every major industry. Richard Beckhard has recognized him as one of the world's first one hundred change agents.

Mr. Sullivan specializes in the science and art of systematic and systemic change, executive team building, and facilitating Whole System Transformation Conferences—large interactive meetings with 300 to 1,500 people. Over 25,000 people have participated in his conferences worldwide; one co-facilitated with Kristine Quade held for the Amalgamated Bank of South Africa was named runner-up for the title of outstanding change project of the world by the OD Institute.

With William Rothwell and Gary McLean, he is revising one of the field's seminal books, *Practicing OD: A Consultant's Guide* (Jossey-Bass/Pfeiffer, 1995). The first edition is now translated into Chinese.

He did his graduate work in organization development at Pepperdine University and Loyola University.

Mr. Sullivan's current interests include the following: Whole-system transformation, balancing economic and human realities; discovering and collaborating with cutting-edge change-focused authors who are documenting the perpetual renewal of the OD profession; and applied phenomenology: developing higher states of consciousness and self-awareness in the consulting of interdependent organizations.

Mr. Sullivan's current professional learning is available at www.rolandsullivan.com.

 **Kristine Quade** is an independent consultant who combines her background as an attorney with a master's degree in organization development from Pepperdine University and years of experience as both an internal and external OD consultant.

Ms. Quade draws from experiences in guiding teams from divergent areas within corporations and across many levels of executives and employees. She has facilitated leadership alignment, culture change, support system alignment, quality process improvements, organizational redesign, and the creation of clear strategic intent that results in significant bottom-line results. A believer in whole-system change, she has developed the expertise to facilitate groups ranging in size from eight to two thousand in the same room for a three-day change process.

Recognized as the 1996 Minnesota Organization Development Practitioner of the Year, Ms. Quade teaches in the master's programs at Pepperdine University and the University of Minnesota at Mankato and the master's and doctoral programs at the University of St. Thomas in Minneapolis. She is a frequent presenter at the Organization Development National Conference and also at the International OD Congress and the International Association of Facilitators.

Index